Paradigm Shift in Education

Paradigm Shift in Education

Dr.S.K.PANNER SELVAM
Assistant Professor, Department of Education
Bharathidasan University, Tiruchirappalli, T.N
and
Mrs.R.DEVI
Assistant Professor, Merit College of Education,
Ariyalur, T.N

RANDOM

RANDOM PUBLICATIONS

NEW DELHI (INDIA)

Paradigm Shift in Education

ISBN 978-93-5111-531-1

Published in 2015 in India by
RANDOM PUBLICATIONS
4376-A/4B, Gali Murari Lal, Ansari Road
New Delhi-110 002
Phone : +9111-43580356, 011-43142548, 011-23289044
e-mail : sales@randompublications.com
info@randompublications.com
randomexports@gmail.com

Reprinted 2026

Type Setting by : Shah Computer Graphics, Delhi-110094

Contents

15

16

1

A Paradigm Shift in Distance Education: E-learning

Introduction

The world has been in a process of structural transformation for over last twenty years. This multidimensional and structural transformation process is associated with the emergence of a new technological paradigm that is based on information and communication technologies. All organizations are in transition today. Transition in the structures of organizations is the key concept of the 21st century. All organizations and institutions are faced with some significant shifts, resulting from the impact of emerging technologies and a global economy. The source of these shifts can be analyzed by following challenges:

1. Changing patterns of competition, trade and technological innovations

2. Exponential growth of knowledge

3. Worldwide social concerns for general quality of life

4. Global demand for education.

Historical Development Process of Distance Education

Historical development process of distance education environments represents the way that distance learning technologies have evolved through the years. Williams, Pap rock and Covington (1999) indicate the historical development process of distance education environments by using a figure below.

Table -1

LEVEL	MEDIA
Level 3 (1990s) : Highly interactive	Virtual classrooms - Hybrid networks Digital TVInternet- Web-Online videoMultimedia Computer Based Training
Level 2 (1960s) :Passive to moderately - Active	Two-way interactive audio/videoe-mail, computer mediated conferencesComputer based training - Satellite video television
Level 1 (1880s) : Passive	Audio and videotape – RadioCorrespondence

As it can be seen in Table 1, Level 1 is being described as passive distance learning. In this level, the students don't have any chance for interactivity. This type of environment called as asynchronous distance learning environment. Also Level 2 is being characterized as passive to moderately active distance learning. These distance learning environments are synchronous because of the two way interactivity. Finally Level 3 is being defined as highly interactive. Level 3 also consists of hybrid distance learning environments in addition to the capabilities of Internet.

When the historical process of distance education is being observed, it can easily be seen that, there is no single concept of learning through the use of information and communication technologies. Online training, computer assisted learning, web-learning, virtual learning, digital training are the different types of information and communication technologies that can be used in distance education.

e-learning

The term e-learning comprises a lot more than *online learning, virtual learning, distributed learning, networked* or *web-based learning.* As the letter "e" in e-learning stands for the word "electronic", e-learning would incorporate all educational activities that are carried out by individuals or groups working online or offline, and synchronously or asynchronously via networked or standalone computers and other electronic devices. *E-learning* is commonly referred to the intentional use of networked information and communications technology in teaching and learning.

Social software is a kind of software that users can contribute their content, and therefore this content gets richer or more accurate and more people cause it. Social software includes providing mentoring, building community, meeting, and personal learning assistance, reducing communication errors, working collaboratively on projects or problems, and supporting complex group functions. The term of social software is being described as tools which support the social relationships between people using the web. The concept of social software refers the scope of applications which enables social connections, group's interactions, shared web spaces for collaboration and information exchange in web based environments. The term of social software is the major component of Web 2.0.

WEB 2.0

In the 21st century, a series of technological developments are being occurred. One of the new technological developments is called as Web 2.0. This term states renaissance for web resources and tools by containing collaboration and social interaction. Web 2.0 includes community learning and collaborative learning in social process.

E-Learning describes as using of internet technologies for creating and delivering a rich learning environment. This learning environment includes abroad series of solutions, information resources and instruction. The goal of e-Learning is enhancing the individual and the organizational performance. In Web 1.0, students can access the content that created by someone else. However, in Web 2.0, students can design their own content.

Table – 2 : Some Comparative Characteristics of Web 1.0 and Web 2.0

Web 1.0	Web 2.0
Britannica Online	Wikipedia
Personal Websites	Blogging
Content Management Systems	Wikis
Directories (Taxonomy)	Tagging (Folksonomy)

Web 1.0 describes as collection of web sites (read only web sites). Current trends of web technologies and tools are changed today. E-Learning 2.0 and Web 2.0 (read and write web sites) are the popular concepts for all organizations. Styles (2006) stated the paradigm shift that Web 2.0initiated in publication history.

Table – 3 : Evaluation of Web 2.0 and Chance of Publication History

Wikis	✓ With the evaluation of Web 2.0the most popular encyclopaedia is no longer Britannica ✓ Now it is Wikipedia
Podcasting	✓ Podcasting is a key feature of Web 2.0 ✓ People can use their portable players or in -Tunes
Blogs	✓ The concept of blogs are easy to use for publishing ✓ Blogs can receive feedback on ideas before they are published
Really Simple Syndication(RSS)	1. This technology can help people to manage information overload

Web 2.0 represents a new era of paradigm shift. In this era, there is a transition from traditional software to internet services (Bray, 2007).Transition from the traditional view of e-learning to the dimension of technology aiming collaborative nature of learning refers e-Learning 2.0. e-Learning 2.0 contains:

2. Discussion forums
3. Blended learning
4. Virtual classrooms
5. Podcasts
6. Mobile learning
7. Games
8. Blogs,
9. Wikis etc

Individual Requirements for Successful Online Distance Education

For delivery of distance education via the Internet to be successful, a number of individual and organizational requirements must be met.

a) Self-directed learning: Because the foundation of Internet online education is knowledge building rather than knowledge transmission, students must be willing and able to participate in the process of directing and creating their own learning experiences. Online learning requires the student to participate to a much greater extent in the creation of the learning experience, and in return gives the learner greater control over that experience. Network learning .encourages, even requires, active rather than passive learning.

b) Technology and technical skills: To participate effectively in distance education on the Internet, individual students must have access to the appropriate technology, specific computer skills for working with the technologies, and access to training and technical assistance for using the technology. Technical assistance should include online, telephone, and email support on an ongoing basis, preferably 24 hours a day, seven days a week.

c) Communication and collaboration skills: Online education relies heavily on interaction between students and teachers and between students and other students. Thus, in order to successfully participate in a collaborative learning environment, learners must possess appropriate communications skills and will need to be familiar with and able to use various distance based synchronous and asynchronous conferencing tools. Networking technology expands the opportunities for student-to-student communication and provides students with the ability to collaborate with each other as part of the learning experience.

d) Research and information retrieval skills: In order for students to be able to utilize the Internet for online education, they must be able to .maximize the potential of electronic resources. by having knowledge of the structure of the database, being able to use procedures for searching databases, knowing the most useful databases and digital libraries to search, having familiarity with the most useful search engines, and understanding how various resources are linked together. Lack of information retrieval skills can in fact be a major barrier for online students.

Organizational Requirements for Successful Online Distance Education

To ensure success for the online learner, organizations that offer distance education have to provide more than course materials alone. The system should provide extensive support for faculty and for learners. In addition, there are considerations for the organization itself, as online education differs from traditional face-to-face classes, and even from distance education programs of the past.

a) Pedagogical and instructor training and support: Organizations have an obligation to the learner to design a pedagogically sound program, which is clear in objectives, process and evaluation. A properly designed course takes advantage of what the Internet has to offer (interaction, speed, convenience and cross-referencing among different sources) and combines them in optimal ways to meet the learning goals. One of the most important requirements of the organization is a well-trained faculty with an understanding of the pedagogy of distance education.

b) Learner empowerment: The system should allow learners opportunities for collaboration, dialogue, practice, exploration, research, and evaluation. A well-designed system is flexible, adapting to the individual learners needs and abilities. The interface makes navigation simple, while engaging the learner.

c) Interaction: Computer networks provide a means for learners to interact with the

Instructor as well as with each other. Through synchronous and asynchronous communication, students .share and create knowledge together. Thus, the Internet has had a tremendous influence on distance education. Students are now supported in ways that were not possible prior to the advent of computer-mediated communication. Communication among students, teachers and administrators is not only faster, but stronger.

d) Student technical support: A learning system also needs to ensure that learners can receive assistance with and clarification of technical and non-technical aspects. Learners enter the system with varying levels of ability and familiarity with the materials and tools.

e) Online library services: One area that is sometimes overlooked is the library services. Where the traditional university relies on physical holdings, the online organization needs to have digital databases at its disposal. Digital libraries can provide the information a student need, when s/he needs it. They offer all the speed and convenience that the Internet provides. Given the importance of research skills, use of the library is a technical skill that should be taught alongside use of the other tools.

Conclusion

Changing information and communication technologies affect organizational and management structures of institutions. Therefore institutions must reconstruct their organizational structures in view of the technological speed of change as creating flexible and rich learning environments for people. With the gaining speed of technological progress, information and communication technologies are opening up new facilities for learners and learning. Rapid technological progress introduce new terms in recent years. The term paradigm shift is being used often in the 21st century. The paradigm shift in distance education refers to the transition process. New concepts, models and terms are differing from the old ones. Paradigm shift in distance education means substitution of the new educational terms with the old ones. This indicated paradigm shift includes a transition from modern curricula to post-modern curricula and also includes a transition from traditional learning to digitized formats of learning. This paradigm shift is about a shift from tutor centred teaching to a learner centred learning. Audio, video, digital multi-media (including audio, video and incorporating text), texts (including still graphics) and direct (face to face) human contact are the most important media that are used in distance education.

References

1. Anderson, T. (2005). Distance learning – Social software's killer ape? Retrieved: January 03, 2010 from: http
2. Bates, T. (2005). Technology e-learning and Distance Education. (2nd Edition).Network, Rutledge.
3. Bragg, A.B. (2007). Reflections on pedagogy: Reframing Practice to Foster Informal Learning with Social Software. Retrieved: March 20, 2007 from:http://www.dream.sdu.dk/uploads/files/Anne%20Bartlett-Bragg.pdf
4. Bray, T. (2007). Not 2.0? Retrieved: June 24, 2007from: http://radar.oreilly.com/archives/2005/08/not_20.html

5. Cast ells& G. Cardoso (edt.) The Network Society from Knowledge to Policy. Washington, Center for Transatlantic Relations.
6. Cast ells, M. (2004). Informationalism, Networks and the Network Society: A Theoretical Blueprint. Retrieved: March18, 2007 from:http://annenberg.usc.edu/images/faculty/facpdfs/Informationalism.pdf
7. Choy, S. O. & Ng, K.C. (2007). Implementing Wiki Software for Supplementing Online Learning. Australasian Journal of Educational Technology. 23(2), 209-226.
8. Drasil, P &Pitner, T. (2006). e-Learning 2.0: Methodology Technology andSolutions. Retrieved: January 13, 2007 from:http://www.fi.muni.cz/~tomp/l2/e-learning2.0/icte/l2_platform.pdf.
9. Hruby, J & Wooden, J. (2006). Learning 2.0. Applying the Next Generation ofelearning Tools and Techniques. Retrieved: January 13, 2007 from:http://www.fredricksoncommunications.com/Fredrickson_Communications.pdf
10. Khan, B. (2007). Flexible Learning in an Information Society. In: Khan, B. (edt.)Hershey, Information Science Publishing.
11. Peters, O. (2003). Distance Education in Transition. (3rd edition). Verlag: Carlvon Ossietzky University of Oldenburg.
12. Punnie, Y & Cabrera M. (2006). The Future of ICT and Learning in the Knowledge Society. Report on a Joint DG JRC-DG EAC Workshop. Seville, European Commission Joint Research Center.
13. Rosenberg, M.J. (2006). Beyond e-learning: Approaches and Technologies to Enhance Organizational Knowledge, Learning, and Performance. San Francisco:Pfeiffer.75
14. Williams, J. B. & Goldberg, M. (2005). The evolution of e-learning. Retrieved: January 18, 2007 from:http://www.ascilite.org.au/conferences/ /blogs/proceedings/pd

2

Distance Education: Issues, Challenges Andits Future

Introduction

Distance education courses that require a physical on-site presence for any reason (including taking examinations) is considered a hybrid or blended course of study. This emerging technology is becoming widely used in universities and institutions around the globe. With the recent trend of technological advance, distance learning is becoming more recognized for its potential in providing individualized attention and communication with students internationally. Distance learning is a flexible form of learning where a student can study from home, work, on the move or wherever else is convenient.

For those who cannot afford to attend regular classes, distance learning courses have come as blessings. And with the passage of time the initial hesitation of learning through distance education has also gone away. In fact, pursuing a good distance learning course can help a lot of people in scaling high in any organization that they are presently engaged with. Thus apart from allowing you to learn in your own time and pace distance learning also improve your career options. Moreover the course fees of these distance education courses are much lesser as compared to that of the regular courses. As it appears today, the benefits of the correspondence courses will be reaped by more and more people in the future.

History of Distance Learning

The term distance education can be used to describe any of a number of instructional situations. Although it is thought of as a new term, distance learning has been around for well over 100 years. One of the earlier forms of distance learning was done through correspondence courses started in Europe. This stayed the primary means of distance learning until the middle of this century when instructional radio and television became more popular (Imel, 1996). As technology has changed, so has the definition of distance learning. Videotaped lectures have been a standard in university and professional courses for the last two decades (Moore &Lockee, 1998).

Definition

Distance education is defined as "the planned learning that normally occurs in a different place from teaching and as a result requires special techniques of course design, special instructional techniques, special methods of communication by electronic and other technology, as well as special organization and administrative agreements" (Moore and Kearsley1996).

Issues in Distance Learning

Despite the promises and obvious advantages to distance learning, there are certain issues that need to be resolved. These issues include the quality of instruction, hidden costs, misuse of technology, and the attitudes of instructors, students, and administrators. Each one of these has an effect on the overall quality of distance learning as a product. In many ways, each of these issues relates to the others. We will examine each of these issues separately.

Quality of Instruction

The first issue is the quality of instruction that is given through distance learning programmes. Much of the quality of instruction depends on the attitude of the administration and the instructor. Many times it seems that the administration believes the technology itself will improve the quality of the class. Pall off and Pratt (2000) remind us that "technology does not teach students; effective teachers do". They make the point that the issue is not technology itself, but how it is used in the design and delivery of courses.

Cost Effectiveness

The second issue is the true cost and the cost effectiveness of distance learning programs. A study by Phelps et al. (1991) found that "the potential cost-effectiveness of using online technologies in distance education is still uncertain". The study further showed that the concepts of costs and effectiveness are not as simple as they first appear. Atkinson (1983, cited in Ng, 2000) notes, "it is possible for a program to be efficient but not cost effective if the outputs which are actually produced do not contribute to the program objectives: that is it may be efficient at doing the wrong things".

Misuse of Technology

Besides the cost of the technology, there is the possibility of not utilizing all its potential. Some of these problems arise from a lack of training, some from the instructor's attitudes about using the technology, and still others by hardware problems. It seems to be self-evident that instructor needs to be trained to use distance learning technology, but too often they are not. Once again, it appears that administration may feel that the technology itself will improve the course. Advancement in technology does not lead to effective distance education. The best distance education practices depend on creative, well-informed instructors (Greenberg, 1998).

The Role of the Technicians

One overlooked factor in the success or failure of distance learning programmes is the role that the technicians play in distance learning. Of course they play a large role in the technical delivery, but little is known about the non-technical activities of the technicians that could have an influence on the instructional process. In a 1995 study, Olenski et al., found that technicians could indirectly influence the learning environment by "orientating participants to the technology, reducing the anxiety of the participants" (including the instructor), "and by advising the instructor on instructional techniques"

Problems With Equipment

Equipment and hardware malfunctions can be a great detriment to the effectiveness of distance learning. When a problem occurs in a class everything comes to a standstill and the learning environment is interrupted. If there are too many instances, the entire course can be affected. For instance, if an overhead projector goes out during an instructor's presentation, an alternate way of delivering that information can easily be found. However, if a compressed video presentation has problems, the entire class must be stopped until the problem is resolved. If the instructor goes ahead with the lesson, one site will miss out on that information

Attitudes Towards Distance Learning

Despite problems with hardware that may or may not get worked out with new advances in technology, we must come back to instructors and their attitudes towards teaching in a distance-learning environment as a major potential roadblock to effective distance education. As in any educational situation, the instructor can set the tone for learning in the educational environment. That instructor must be properly trained and motivated to be effective. An instructor must have technological skills and confidence to use all of the various electronic devices in order to be truly effective in the electronic classroom. Instructors must also change the manner in which information is delivered. While lecture does not work well, multimedia presentations are successful.

Instructor Concerns

Instructors have other concerns about distance learning, primarily how it will change their role in education. Clark (1993) found in a national survey of attitudes of higher education faculty that there was a moderately positive attitude about distance learning in general, but moderately negative attitudes about their own use of it.

Future Perspectives

For governments the main potential is to increase the capacity and cost- effectiveness of education and training systems, to reach target groups with limited access to conventional education and training, to support and enhance the quality and relevance of existing educational structures, to ensure the connection of educational institutions and curricula to the emerging networks and information resources, and to promote innovation and opportunities for lifelong learning.

Conclusion

What may we conclude from the issues and challenges of distance learning? Are there possibilities for improvement in the future? The technology will undoubtedly keep improving and the price will drop, as technology is prone to do once it comes into general use. Already we see improvement in the delivery systems of compressed video and computer assisted instruction. Despite student problems with distance learning, studies indicate they are relatively satisfied with what they are receiving.

In spite of the need for improvement, the future of distance learning seems bright. Increasing numbers of students enrolling in distance learning classes underscore the need for "comprehensive and thoughtful evolution of distance education if it is to become the educational model of the future" (Harner, et al., 2000,).

References

1. Clark, T. (1993). Attitudes of higher education faculty toward distance education: A national survey. *The American Journal of Distance Education, 7,* 19-33.

2. Greenberg, G. (1998). Distance education technologies: Best practices for K-12 settings. *IEEE Technology and Society Magazine,* (Winter) 36-40.

3. Harner, M., et al. (2000). Measuring the effect of distance education on the learning experience: Teaching accounting via Picturetel. *International Journal of Instructional Media, 27* (1), 37-50.

4. Imel, S. (1998). *Myths and realities of distance learning.* Columbus, Ohio: ERIC Clearinghouse on Adult, Career, and Vocational Education. Ohio State University. (Eric Document Reproduction Service No. ED 414 446).

5. Moore, D.R., &Lockee, B.B. (1998). Taxonomy of bandwidth: considerations and principles to guide practice in the design and delivery of distance education. Unpublished manuscript: Portland State University.

6. Ng, K. (2000). Costs and effectiveness of online courses in distance education. *Open Learning, 15* (3) 301-308.

7. Olesinski, R. et al. (1995). *The operating technician's role in video distance learning.* Paper presented at the Instructional Technology SIG, San Francisco, California. (ERIC Document Reproduction Service No. ED 387 123).

8. Phelps, R.H. et al. (1991). Effectiveness and costs of distance education using computer-mediated communication. *American Journal of Distance Education, 5* (3), 7-19.

9. Palloff, R., & Pratt, K. (2000). *Making the transition: Helping teachers to teach online.* Paper presented at EDUCAUSE: Thinking it through. Nashville, Tennessee. (ERIC Document Reproduction Service No. ED 452 806).

3

The Role of New Media in Distance Education

Introduction

The invention of digital electronics has accelerated the development of technologies over the past 50 years. The use of technology is to aid the processing and communication of information in a new format. The convergence of technology is a vital recent development concerned mainly with the processing of information with that which deals mainly with its communication. It is obviously seen in the emergence of internet through which the processing power in each office and school can easily be connected, and can communicate with corresponding systems anywhere else in the world. When the integration is realized then the distinctions become blurred. Once this point is achieved then the source of information and destination point is become insignificant but the message takes the center stage.

Internet Usage

The usage of internet in education is obvious today. It has been seen that the use of internet in the sphere of organization and educational institutions lead to the increased use of education accessibility on the global scenario and in turn it leads to economic growth and efficiency of institutions. The first world countries extensively use internet development in the sphere of education. The developing countries, despite difficulties, problems and concerns, seek as far as possible to take part in the formation of the global educational community. In doing so, the systematization and analysis of the experience of Internet usage in education becomes a timely issue for each country and the global community as a whole.

Considering the huge scale of the Internet into account, the invention of mechanisms designed for effective navigation of the internet, and the collection, analysis, exchange and distribution of information for the specific use of education gains importance. However, despite the stupendous progress made in some countries in the creation of universal information retrieval systems and specialized information systems for education, neither set of systems taken separately can provide a complete and comprehensive service. It has been noted that a few of current Internet applications are used in most educational institutions. The reason for this situation is from a lack of information rather than a lack of finance.

The current scenario seeks for a solution which can however be provided on the basis of the co-operation and exchange of information between such systems. The specialized information system "Education via the Internet" within the framework of UNESCO programme activity may become one of a group of permanent international tools of co-operation (UNESCO, 2000).

The application of the Internet in education is understood as the use of various Internet technologies for the solution of various educational tasks, namely, teaching, learning and management of the educational process. The systematic analysis of experiences they have been identified and defined in using the Internet in education provides an opportunity for comparison and generalization.

Learning Based on Internet

The internet renders a worldwide forum which to offers curriculum and courses. One can assume, for example, that each student at any time has an excellent encyclopedia at his or her disposal. Course material can be updated. Course text, examples and exercises can be interactive in the sense of immediately demonstrating equations with graphs, changing parameters and seeing the results, linking to other web sites according to the interests of the student. The web based learning model is essentially free from limitations of space and time while it reaches students around the globe.

In addition, the web-based learning model offers the aspiring students an ocean of information that was never possible in the days past. For example, the student who suddenly becomes interested in what kind of art that was drawn during Michelangelo's lifetime could link to that information, even though the instructor may not know how to answer such a doubt. The possibility of connecting to information worldwide in a multitude of formats creates a remarkably rich medium for learning. Web based course work is not merely an electronic duplicate of the original course material. It represents a new type of educational materials which takes full advantage of the emerging web and multimedia technologies in order to achieve an effective yet enjoyable learning process. Thus, complex concepts are introduced in innovative ways. Connecting to vast resources available worldwide introduces new levels of value to the courseware. A web based course offering is envisioned as a dynamically evolving resource that will prove beneficial to both students and instructors alike.

In the light of these foregoing remarks, it is evident that the design of a web based course is a multifarious process that closely resembles that of movie making in video productions. That is, a web based course is developed through the efforts of a team of professionals with a complementary range of skills, as opposed to classical course design, which is typically developed by faculty alone.

The richness of modern web and multimedia technologies allow for unlimited creativity when it comes to electronic courseware development. Such richness gives teachers new opportunities to develop very interesting course material while it also poses a substantial challenge in that it requires faculty to rethink their own course offerings in the light of the new technologies.

Setting A New Educational Platform

One among the areas that requires change is higher education's perception of technology as it relates to its mission. In the recent past most attempts to use technology in higher education have been very haphazard: systems have been designed only to automate existing processes, computers have been thought of as strictly computational devices, and desktop workstations have not accomplished much more than replacing the typewriter and the adding machine.

Today technology is creating a new educational platform and is reconfiguring the modality of student learning process. Learning through network, accessing libraries, scholars, networks, and information worldwide is evolving. In the light of this, one important quarry that needs to be considered what is the mission of higher education? It can be said that education is a discovery process, and its mission is to provide the widest repertoire of possibilities for a student entering a learning situation. Technology can realize this ambition, and because of it a student's educational experience can be immeasurably sound.

Various typologies of Internet Applications in Education (IAE) have been proposed. Two main approaches to the segmentation of this project domain have been revealed through the analysis of recent experience. The technology oriented approach is the most widespread. For example, statistical research on the use of the electronic communication in open and distance learning, conducted by UNESCO in 1995 (Euler and Berg, 1998), has identified the different types of applied telecommunication media in educational programmes like Telephone; Fax; Audio-conference; Video-conference; Electronic mail; and Access to databases.

Ellsworth (1994) proposes the classification of Internet tools in accordance with the types of interaction between the participants in the educational process as follows, interaction between the students and professors in the educational process, interaction between the students and professors while searching for information on the net, joint activities of professors and the administration, students' joint research projects.

Individualized Learning and Teaching

One should not underestimate the prevalence and importance of "person-to- person" (interactive) type of communications on the net. For a long time electronic mail has remained the only internet application in education. Data submitted in the above-mentioned UNESCO survey reveals that electronic mail is still the most frequently used computer technology in open and distance learning (Euler and Berg, 1998).

A relatively new phenomenon in educational communications is the newly established practice of learners speaking directly to experts in one or another field (which can already be considered as a consequence of the increase in the level of communication skills among learners actively using the Internet). On the net, there are a number of domains such as Yahoo! Yahooligans! School Bell; Homework Answers; and Ask a Scientist. By addressing enquiries to these centers learners can receive, via e-mail, answers to their questions on a particular theme.

Group Learning and Teaching Via The Internet

In the internet the lecture or presentation of teaching material published, becomes accessible to many learners. There are electronic discussion and electronic bulletin board which offer coursing materials and they are "read-only" access for the students. It is also interaction in process. This information becomes common and source of information to all the learners.

Conclusion

The advantages offered by the internet in the organization of co-operation are suggested by its very nature. It was created as an environment specifically designed for discursive work on documents by groups of researchers far away from each other. The further development of internet technologies has paved way for the opportunity for joint use and the editing of textual materials, and also of audio and visual sequences.

Concerns of public control and content are of a general problem. It is identified as trans-cultural nature of the net. It presents umpteen challenges for the cultural identity of the nation. It is also multimedia in nature. Institutions do make the best of the available information from the net for the betterment and enhancement of the education.

The internet offers a specialized distance education for all class of people. It also has its own issues and concerns of quality of the education. It is made easy for all in the higher education and it is gradually gaining its place in the high schools.

References

1. UNESCO (2001): Teacher Education through Distance Learning, Technology – Curriculum – Evaluation – Cost, Paris: UNESCO
2. Euler M and Von Berg D (1998): The Use of Electronic Media in Open Learning and

Distance Education, Paris: UNESCO

3. Ellsworth, J.H. (1994): Education on the Internet, Indianapolis: Sams Publishing
4. Daniel, J. S. (1997): Mega-universities and Knowledge Media, Technology Strategies for Higher Education, London: Kogan Page
5. Perraton, H (Ed.) (1993): Distance Education for Teacher Training. London and New York: Routledge

4

Instructional Strategies in Distance Education

Introduction

Classroom teachers rely on number of virtual and unobtrusive cues from their students to enhance their delivery of instructional content. A quick glance, for example, reveals who is attentively taking notes, pondering a difficult concept or preparing to make a comment. The student is frustrated, confused, tired, or bored is equally evident. The attentive teacher consciously and subconsciously receives and analyses these visual cues and adjust the course delivery to meet the needs of the class during the particular lessons. Hence it is easy to enhance student's achievement in face-to-face, real classroom situation.

In contrast, a distant teacher has few, if any, visual cues. Those cues that do exist are filtered through technological devices such as video monitors. It is difficult to carry on a stimulating teacher class discussion when spontaneity is altered by technical requirements and distance. Without the use of real time visual medium such as television, the teacher receives no visual information from the distant sites. The teacher might never really know, for example, if students are asleep, talking among themselves or even in the room. Separation by distance also affects the general rapport of the class. Leaving in different communities, geographic regions or even states deprive the teacher and students of a common community link. Hence utmost importance should be given to enhance the student's achievement in distance education. This can be done by using different strategies of instruction in distance education.

Instructional Strategies

Instructional strategies are those tactics used by the instructor to promote learning. According to Smith, B.O "The strategy means the determination of some policy by planning before presenting the contents with the help of which the student's force is faced and the teaching objectives are achieved".

To enhance the student's achievement in distance education following strategies can be used:

1. Taking students readiness into account

- Course orientation quizzes covering course requirements. First lesson reviewed basic concepts. Students are introduced first to concepts of distance learning as a prelude to course content.
- From welcome screen students move to syllabus. The acceptance of the syllabus document is an assigned requirement, which confirms students understand expectations.
- Programme should be step-by-step approach moving from simplest concepts to most complicate.

2. Defining instructional expectations

- Initial face-to-face or videoconference meeting. Expectations are restated in email to the students.

- Classroom profile section provides listing of completed activities. Step by step instruction specifying what procedures students was to follow within the course.

3. Providing team work instructional strategies

- Encourage collaboration and discussion; refer to responses, synthesize responses, provide information, offer insight, offer additional input and provide opposite perspective from participants and ask them to think about and redirect response.
- Threaded discussion; continual collaborative feedback enhances active learning socially, not competitively, prevents isolation of student. Assign person to lead and to start activity.
- Provide tools for groups to give and receive constructive feedback including instructions to do so and examples of good feedback.

4. Providing reminders strategies

- Mnemonic devices should be used; highlighted words represented terms in glossary or were links to maps are examples. Examples should be used that illustrated application of learning at real world. Weekly audiovisual updates with PowerPoint and email.

5. Providing of transfer of learning instructions

- Assignments should be given in "building block" format. Modules are related to previous modules and drawn from previous knowledge. Directed to additional or previous material to problem solves.
- Students describe in discussion threats how current learning is relevant in their own lives.

- Project sheets direct students to learn an objective, and then apply to real world situations.

6. Utilizing repetition effectively

- Important information should be repeated several times and in several locations.
- Varying activities to reinforce learning followed reading; graphics and pictures repeat concepts.
- Units should be broken down into lessons. Summary ties all together at the end of the unit.

7. Clarifying communication

- Multimedia should provide stimulation to participation and engage different learning styles.
- Format of class including quiz schedule, projects, attendance policy, supplemental material to lecture, video presentations, access to college library, requirement for communication.
- Videotaped lectures in adjunct to online course; weekly audiovisual updates with PowerPoint and email.
- Instructor should take an active role in threaded discussions; frequent clarifying questions to eliminate confusion and encourage participation.

8. Providing subject matter unifiers

- Models and diagrams should be used and developed by students; problem based/knowledge based environment to create higher level of thinking.
- Rich in research design and format- related links metaphors, recommended readings.

9. Keeping students on task

- Weekly agenda with list of assignments, instructional activities and evaluation.
- Tasks should be performed in the field and then reported into website. Teacher is not with them during the field tasks. Tasks had to meet a timeline.

10. Providing ample learning time

- A major question should be posted in one day of the week and must be answered by noon Mondays.
- Assignments and tasks should be posted in the beginning of the course, as were due dates.

11. Improving interaction and feedback

- Arrange telephone office hours using a toll-free number. Set evening office hours if most of the student working during the day.
- Contact each site (students) every week if possible, especially early in the course. Take note of students who do not participate during the first session, and contact them individually after the class.
- Use an onsite facilitator to stimulate interaction when distant students are hesitant to ask questions or participate. In addition, the facilitator can act as you onsite "eyes and ears."

Conclusion

The instructional strategies are energizers of the distance learning. By following the above mentioning strategies not only the online teacher of distance education but also a teacher in face-to-face environment can enhance the student's achievement. The phenomenal growth of distance learning systems all over the world has drastically changed the educational scenario everywhere today. Distance education has been viewed by many as a viable strategy to achieve to national educational goals quickly and at low costs.

References

1. Friedman, M.I. and Fisher, S.P. (1998) *Handbook on Effective Instructional Strategies: Evident for Decision-making.* Institute for Evidence - Based Decision-Making in Education, Inc: Columbia, SC.

2. P. Renga, Ramanugam (2005) *Distance Open Learning Challenges to Developing Countries:* Shipra Publications, New Delhi.

3. Sharma, R.N. and Chandra, S.S. (2003) *Advanced Educational Technology.* Atlantic Publishers and Distributors. New Delhi

5

Challenges in Distance Education in 21st Century

Distance education is student- oriented and exactly what the term implies- any type of study that takes place when the instructor and the student(s) are separated by physical distance, with printed materials and various technologies used for communication and program delivery.

Distance education has traversed four to five 'generations' of technology in its history. These are print, audio/ video broadcasting, audio/ video teleconferencing, computer aided instruction, e-learning/ online learning, computer broadcasting etc.

The emergence of the distance education system is obviously an inevitable development in the evolution of education. The inherent inadequacy of the conventional education system to accommodate the ever increasing frontiers of knowledge and the tremendous increase in the number of aspirants for higher education has led to the emergence of distance education all over the world. It has assumed universal recognition for its ability to extend educational opportunities to all and widen the access for the sake of equity through its innovative and flexible strategies. It is now commonly believed to be a 'wave of future' with unlimited possibilities where conventional main stream higher education does not have sufficient to deliver.

Distance education has nearly opened a new window of opportunities for those who desire for further studies. In a way it has helped numerous professionals, dropouts (school & college), housewives, etc to all accomplish their unfinished dreams. It has immense relevance, particularly in a country like India, where pursuing education is a pricey affair.

The whole purpose of providing distance education is to provide cost-effective, quality education to large sections of our populations including those living in remote and far flung areas. Distance education helps in dissemination of knowledge to people. Multimedia approach in distance education has made it more learners friendly and cost effective. A diversity of target group can be identified and trained through distance mode.

The physical infrastructure and financial expense incurred in a traditional learning centre are far more as compared to those required for educating masses through distance mode. Today's distance education course makes use of E-mail, the web, and video conferencing over broadband network connections for both wired physical locations and wireless mobile learning

Challenges facing Distance Education in the 21st Century

1. To Gear up to meet the increasing demand for quality higher education at low cost.
2. Lack of entry qualifications.
3. Remote location or remote students
4. Among women, deprived and economically poor candidate enrolment.
5. Perseverance in studies.

6. Dropout rate reduction.
7. Use of diverse technologies.
8. Impact or nature of support systems.
9. Meet the global standard.
10. Emergence of ICT (cost effective) also.
11. Mercerization
12. Blurring boundaries between DE and conventional Universities.
13. Identifying target population.
14. Role of academic faculty.
15. Budgeting.
16. Language of instruction.
17. Effective and quality higher education.
18. Designing global market.

Teaching Style and Mode of Operation

1. Different teaching styles.
2. Different instructional methods.
3. Flexibility (adjustments).
4. Upgrading to digital age.
5. Focus on professional degrees.
6. More practical oriented (giving training in use of the tools).
7. Counselling and guidance cells.
8. Challenging the industries with high quality distance education.

9. Usage of mobile technologies.
10. Employment of digital technologies.
11. Losing the content in the name of technology.
12. Identification of competitors (local, national& international).
13. Identification of co operative parties.
14. Promoting collaboration (academic, training and employment).
15. Meet the mass population.
16. Increase regional focus.
17. Single or dual mode operation.
18. Blended mode.

Challenges Ahead in Support System

19. Faculty payment.
20. Fee structure.
21. Providing sophisticated infrastructure in the support sectors (like on campus user).
22. Skill up gradation by faculty from time to time.
23. Gap between education and employment.
24. Increased student's mobility
25. Application oriented research.
26. Innovations in practical teaching.
27. Provide relevant and advanced information.
28. Promotion of inter disciplinary teaching and research.

Internal and External Evaluation

29. Program and course accreditation.

30. Faculty evaluation.

31. Support system evaluation.

32. Successful programs revaluation.

33. Creation of knowledge connectivity map across the country (e-journal, edusat&infonet).

34. Quality control measurement

Conclusion

All the above challenges have to be met and therefore distance education can match the academic programmes with direct employment needs which grown exponentially now a days. Thus Distance education in Indian higher education is undergoing architectural changes.

6

Challenges in Distance Education in 21st Century

Education through distance mode is gaining premium currency in the 21st Century despite the exponential growth of educational institutions and enrolment of students in these institutions. Distance education provides a vast and wide access to higher education by exploiting technological advancements. The premise of this article is identification of the challenges in Distance Education and overcoming the challenges in a coordinated manner. Distance education has changed from an anomaly to a standard component of most higher education institutions. Through the delivery of courses on-line, via the internet, or through satellite or television broadcasts, colleges and universities have found it profitable to provide learning services and opportunities through alternative delivery methods.

There is no doubt that mobile technology may increase possibilities for efficient interaction between distance students, making them more independent of time and space. The total integration of distance education IT systems is in our view the major prerequisite for operating efficient and effective large-scale distance education, including a mobile learning environment (Paulsen et al, 2003).

One of the overall aims when engaging in mobile learning projects has been to extend the distribution of learning materials and communication solutions to lighter equipment and to increase the flexibility in distance education, i.e. refining the total distance learning environment to meet the needs of the *'mobile distance learner'* (Rekkedal et al. 2003). Leaning is most effective when it is a student's full time-time job (Egbokhare, 2006 quoting Rosen field, 2000), this is the more reason why quality of programmes must be maintained in order to at least produce a justified learning outcomes.

Distance Education: An overview

For teachers, Distance Education provides new teaching opportunities online or through correspondence. For students, Distance Education provides an alternative way to continue their schooling. For the working or busy adult, distance education provides the opportunity to pursue a higher education while not giving up their jobs.

Due to the popularity of Distance Education over the years many more colleges and universities are offering Distance Education to students along with traditional in-class schooling. Schools are set up to deliver Distance Education in one of two ways: asynchronous or synchronous instruction. The future for Distance Education seems reassuring and promising.

Un-precedence technological innovations in communications have pushed distance education approaches to the forefront of educational practice. The distance learner can now have almost the same instructional contact and interaction as the student on campus. In fact, the proliferation of the modem, teleconferencing, and the World Wide Web provide a rich expanse of both information and contacts that were previously unavailable.

Problems and Challenges of Distance Education

Distance learning is student-centered learning; thus knowing the characteristics and demographics of the distance learners helps us understand the potential barriers to leaning. Student motivation has a powerful effect on attrition and completion rates, regardless of institutional setting. Motivators for adult distance students are often different from those of traditional students. Knowles (1980), in explaining the advantages of knowing the learner, believes that learner behavior is influenced by a combination of the learner's needs plus the learner's situation and personal characteristics.

Challenges

- Loss of student motivation due to the lack of face-to-face contact with teachers and peers
- Effective use of the technologies
- Feelings of alienation and isolation
- The instructional delivery is based on variables such as: instructor ability, climate of learning, learner attitudes about the experience, etc
- Providing additional support for faculty development of course materials (i.e., visuals, written materials, etc.)
- Making the quality of the programme a high priority
- Learner responsibility and dedication
- Providing incentives and rewards to faculty for the involvement and dedication (faculty recognition or compensation for innovative and creative efforts)
- Administrative assistance or responsibility, and what administrators and their units can do to foster program effectiveness and overall quality
- Developing new courses and workshops to respond to industry changes and trends
- Continual updating of course content
- Committing energies and resources
- Pre-service faculty development specifically for distance education teaching
- Promoting distance education techniques as a method of complementing the academic department's mission
- Assuring cost-competitiveness
- Providing for sufficient planning timelines
- Raising the standards of teacher qualifications, and continuing professional development of teachers
- Increasing educational equity
- Faculty evaluation of programmes, course evaluation and programme accreditation.
- Lack of student training, particularly in reference to technical issues.

Distance Education teachers need to be ready to face challenges different than those offered by traditional classes as well as need to approach courses with a different teaching style. These barriers can be mitigated through technological methods such as e-mail. Computer conferencing and electronic mail can be integrated into the delivery of the course to provide the missing interactivity. Careful attention must be paid to the quality of the material presented in distance courses. Curriculums and assessment materials must be developed that equal that of the traditional classroom if distance courses are to receive the respect they deserve. Maintain the same course content, learning objectives, standards, and credits for all sections, regardless of method of delivery. Assessing student performance is a problem area in distance learning. It is a commonly held belief that distance students perform more poorly in assessment than do internal students because of the additional pressures and burdens of distance study

References

1. Knowles, M. (1980). The Modern Practice of Adult Education: From Pedagogy to Androgogy. Chicago: Follett Publishers.
2. Egbokhare, F.O. (2006): Quality Assurance in Distance Learning In Olayinka, A.I and Adetimirin, V.O (eds) (2006) Quality Assurance in Higher Education. Proceedings of a Symposium to mark The African University Day, 2005 Postgraduate School, University of Ibadan, Nigeria.
3. Odejide, A.I (2007). Quality and Relevance in University of Ibadan's General Studies Programme. A Public Lecture to commemorate the General Studies Programme's Twenty-First Anniversary of University of Ibadan, Nigeria. 27.3.2008. *Scandinavian perspective*. Bekkestua: NKI
4. Paulsen, M. F. 2007: COGs, CLIPs and Other Instruments to Support Cooperative Learning in Virtual Learning Environments.Bernath, U. &Sangrà, A. (eds.): Research on

competence development in online distance education and e-learning - Selected papers from the 4th EDEN Research Workshop in Castelldefels/Spain, October 25 – 28, 2006, pp 109 – 126. Oldenburg: BIS-Verlag.

5. Rekkedal, T., Qvist-Eriksen, S., Fagerberg, T., Paulsen, M. F., Aakre, A. K. &Sjaastad. J. 2003: Student Support Services in E-learning, http://www.nettskolen.com/forskning/student_support/student_support.pdf Retrieved 1.6.2007.

7

The Open and Distance Learning, "Integrating Group-self Evaluation System"

Introduction

In a university programme concerned with learning and teaching in higher education, an important component is in the form of a group presentation. In Open and Distance Learning (ODL), a very important component of the study skills is group discussion. This involves self, peer, and group participations. Learning experiences of students can be enhanced through individual, peer or group-self assessment of assignments, projects and or tests. Much recent literature on assessment in higher education gives strong support to the use of both group and self- assessment.

They are colored with biases and abuses which tend to make the evaluation invalid and unreliable. The point being made is that the learner should be involved in the assessment of his educational achievement. Some researchers have questioned the effectiveness of this method of developing test instruments and in helping students develop real understanding. But Scott et al (2003), confirm that it is a proven method to teach both understanding and problem- solving which use fairly complex problems that require conceptual understanding and a systematic attack and to explicitly teach and coach good problem-solving strategies and appraisal of the quality of instruction and overall effectiveness of teaching and learning. Group- self-evaluation activities can be a useful and valuable avenue in helping students promote personal and academic growth including developing their critical skills in the evaluation process. It results in their consciously improving how they learn. If we want teachers to be more objective and less personally involved in the outcomes of learning than the students are, it becomes very necessary to encourage group- self assessment in our school system especially in the ODL system. The need for students to practice self- assessment arises in order to improve the quality of their objective work. To Curtz (2006), the practice of self- assessment is a central way for students to acquire the reflective habits of mind which are essential to their ongoing capacities to do good work and to progressively improve their work overtime. This will bring about growth in intelligence or thinking, which is precisely growth in the capacity for ongoing reflective self- assessment.

Benefits of Group- Self Evaluation

There are so many benefits derivable from the use of group- self-evaluation in our school system. According to Langan and Wheater (2003), the potential benefits are:

- An educational process that installs autonomy in learners.
- Empowerment of the learner in a learning environment.
- Development of learners 'confidence in assessment/ marking (through practice).
- Developments of learners to self- evaluate and reflect.
- Clear, open marking systems (seeing what is required and improving work).

- Encourages students to critically analyze work done by them and others, rather than simply seeing a mark.
- Several groups can be run at the same time as not all the groups require the presence of the teacher.

For Boud (1995), self-assessment is a transferable skill and is a principal part of the students 'learning experience. And to Brown and Knights (1994), students will be expected to practice self-evaluation in everyday life and in every area of their lives on graduation. It is a good exercise in self-development to ensure that their abilities are extended. Witson (2002), listed a number of perceived advantages as:

- Students have more ownership of the assessment process.
- It can involve students in devising and understanding assessment criteria and in making judgment.
- It encourages formative assessment- learning through feedback.
- It is expected in working situations.
- It encourages intrinsic rather than extrinsic motivation.
- It challenges the role of the teacher as the sole arbiter of assessment.

The Concept of Open and Distance Learning

Open and Distance Learning refers to educational patterns, approaches and strategies that permit people to learn with no barriers in respect of time and space, age and previous educational qualification-no entry qualification, no age limit, no regards to sex, race, tribe, state of origin etc. (Alaezi, 2005). According to Jegede (2005), it has developed from a modest and inconsequential beginning through correspondence courses to a full-fledged modern day technology-facilitated, flexible and learner driven, self-directed learning which involves learners who are often in locations remote from the institutions and/or the instructional or tutorial facilitators. ODL is a composite concept. This is because it is made up of two components. These are Open learning and Distance Education. According to Holmberg (1997), it is a system of education that does not operate through convention which is essentially restrictive in nature-admission restriction, attendance restrictions, subject combination restrictions among others. On the other hand, Distance Education lays emphasis on the physical distance which does not permit direct interaction between the teacher and the learner. The combination of Distance Education and Open Learning will give a composite picture in the context of the term-Open and Distance Learning.

According to Otto-Peters (1993), this composite picture can be viewed when we take ODL as a special form of education in which:

- Teachers and students work apart from each other, i.e. at a distance.
- Printed materials are exchanged with the aid of a mailing system.
- Learning usually takes place in the students' home.
- Learning and learning processes allow a degree of openness with regards to access, age , goals, methods, duration, location among others.

ODL provides affordable, cost effective and flexible educational opportunities for all. It accommodates diverse learning styles. It provides access to remote and naturally inaccessible and under-represented groups. It meets the specific and special educational needs of variety of learners. It also dwells and thrives on economies of scale. It is highly recommended as an avenue to learning in ways most appropriate, efficient and effective to the individual learners. They turn to ODL largely for convenience. They are highly motivated to succeed. They are disciplined to incorporate study time into their busy daily lives. Some of the characteristics as itemized by Rowntree (2008) are:

- Mostly from 35—49 years old (some are more some are less).
- Come from a variety of organizations including public sector, but a few have no job.
- Some seek to develop work skills, others to prove themselves.
- A few have degrees but most have A-levels or less.
- Most have relevant experience, e.g. of being managed or of managing children or family budgets.
- Some have partners who are unsupportive.
- Most see the study skills as rusty or undeveloped.
- Most have done no systematic studying since leaving school.

Integrating the group- self-evaluation in the ODL system ODL, More than most other kinds of learning, often claims to be learner-centred. Many people come to the educational arena with different backgrounds and experiences. People's lives run in different ways. Therefore, the educational and training situation has become segmented and diversified. ODL providers now face new demands from a greater varieties of learners- more matured ones. These learners have rights as well as responsibilities. We have to agree to think of our learners in ODL as our partners in learning. This means that for us to focus instruction on the total development of the learner, he must be seriously involved in all aspects of the instruction including assessment and evaluation. Considering the characteristics of the learners in the ODL system and the benefits derivable from the use of group- self assessment of learning outcomes, it becomes necessary to integrate group- self assessment in the ODL system. This is because ODL is democratic and learner- centred. Therefore this should be extended to the assessment process in ODL. The learners are matured and responsible enough to express their capacity for reflective assessment.

Conclusion

The modern world is moving towards democratization and liberalization of educational opportunities through the use of open learning and/or ODL. Therefore educational should not be left out. It should be democratized, through group- self-evaluation. This is because of its mutuality. Everybody should judge. Everybody is judged.

References

1. Akinjobi, A. (1982). Why WAEC fails the Test Every Year. Lagos. Sunday Times. January 17, (p. 5).
2. Alaezi, O. (2005). National Open University Plan: Enhancing High Education in Nigeria through ODL Delivery Systems. Lagos. NOUN.
3. Angelo, T. (2000), Classroom Assessment: Guildlines for Success. Teaching Excellence towards the Best in the Academy. 12(4), 1- 2.North Miami Beach. FL. The Professional and organizational Devel Network in Higher Education. Essays on Teaching Excellence Series.
4. Boud, D. (1995). Enhancing Learning through Self-Assessment. London. Kogan page. Brown, S. and Knights, P. (1994). Assessing Learning in Higher Education. London.
5. Kogan Page. Brown, G., Bull, J.andPendlebury, M. (1997). Assessing Students in Higher Education. London.
6. Holmberg, B. (1997). Status and Trends of Distance Education. London, Kogan Page. Institute of Interactive Media and Learning (2004), Peer Assessment. http://ahe.cqu,edu.au/self peergroup.htm
7. Lewis, K.O.(2006). Evaluation of Online Group Activities: Intra-Group Member Peer Evaluation. http://www.uwex.edu/disted/conference
8. Looksmart, M. (2008). Innovate: Learning at a distance. Engaged or not. http://www.furt.net

9. Otto-Peters (1993), Understanding Distance Education. American Journal of Distance, Education 27, 3. 11-21.

10. Rowntree (2008). Who are your Distance Learners. Distance Learners. http://iet.open.ac.uk/pp/D.G.F.Rowntree/distance-learning.htm

11. Scott, W. B., Duan, L.D. and Robert,J.B. (2003). Comparism of Students Performance Using Web and Paper Based Home work in College Level Physics. Journal of Research in Science and Teaching. Vol. 40, No. 10. (p. 1000- 1071).

8

Academic Challenges in Distance Education

Distance Education: A Closer Look

Distance education is a creative method of applying electronic technology to teaching and learning and to provide a wider access to higher education.

For teachers, Distance Education provides new teaching opportunities online or through correspondence. For students, Distance Education provides an alternative way to continue their schooling. For the working or busy adult, distance education provides the opportunity to pursue a higher education while not giving up any of their habits or responsibilities.

Due to the popularity of Distance Education over the years (i.e., since the late 1990s), many more colleges and universities are offering Distance Education to students in addition to traditional in-class schooling.

Distance Education in India

The Distance Learning in India programmed presented at institutions in India can be categorized under the some disciplines, which are Arts, Science and Commerce. Students can choose for both undergraduate, post graduate degrees, doctorate degrees as well as diploma course and certificate courses. A lot of universities in India have a section for distance education that presented courses in various streams. The Open Universities situated in the different states in India present distance learning programs to students all over the country.

Distance Education system basically relates to correspondence courses wherein the students are not attending regular classes and yet continue their studies. However, the course contents, duration, mode of examination and Degree awarded are the same as applicable to regular students. The academic activities include teaching material supplied in regular instalments, evaluation of response sheets and personal contact programmer and/or Radio Teaching.

Distance Learning Tips

To succeed in distance education, students must be willing to learn on their own with little guidance. It is important to stay with the class or ahead, not behind. Finding the appropriate environment for studying and setting aside time for studying are essential for online students: since there is no physical time in class, in fact, students need to respect deadlines to do the required reading and complete assignments as well as actively participate to online discussions, ask questions, and make replies weekly.

Distance education also requires an extra effort from teachers who need to be available for e-questions throughout the day and need to provide a clear course syllabusor outline to guide students through the course.

Academic Challenges in Distance Education

Distance Education, however, also has its drawbacks for learning, colleges and universities, teachers, parents, and students.

Academic Challenges in Distance Education Learning

There seems to be many questions concerning Distance Education: Is the quality of the teaching and learning as well as experience of a Distance Education student as good as in a traditional classroom? Does Distance Education meet expectations? And, does Distance Education provide professional development for students? Such questions as these reveal academic challenges in distance education that must be resolved when offering programs fully online.

Academic Challenges in Distance Education for Colleges and Universities

Whether or not the quality of education provided by Distance Education is comparable to that of traditional courses is an ongoing debate for school accreditors. To become accredited distance education schools, institutions must periodically undergo an accreditation visit and be reviewed to determine if they meet the criteria needed for accreditation (i.e., be either national or regionally accredited). Accreditors also check to see if the distance education provides sufficient, reliable, and valuable learning environment for students.

According to the U.S. Department of Education, "the goal of accreditation is to ensure that education provided by institutions of higher education meets acceptable levels of quality."

Academic Challenges in Distance Education for Teachers

Distance Education teachers need to be ready to face challenges different than those offered by traditional classes as well as need to approach courses with a different teaching style. Teachers who post schoolwork online need to learn for themselves how to use one of a variety of course management systems including Web CT, Blackboard, Top Class, and so on. As well, teachers are required to pay particular attention to the creation of a syllabus that needs to guide students through the course. Plus, teachers are often faced with having to develop distance education tests and lectures that are effective when delivered through the Internet.

With Distance Education, teachers need to be available for students several times a week, if not every day, at any hour the day to answer student questions or provide assistance (just to name a few, reasons). Also, there are academic challenges for faculty involvement and instructional support when Distance Education students encounter troubles. Furthermore, Distance Education teachers need to check often for students' online schoolwork, assignments, papers, tests, as well as any else sent in via correspondence mail.

Academic Challenges in Distance Education for a Student's Parents

Parents of Distance Education students face uncertainty as they might be unsure of whether the quality of schooling provided by distance education can be comparable to classroom learning. They might think their Distance Education student may not teach as much as a traditional student who attends traditional classes.

Academic Challenges in Distance Education for Students

Distance Education students should know that distance education requires them to be self-disciplined and responsible to meet course requirements. At times, Distance Education students are faced with academic challenges (and constraints) as they continue to live their lives as part time students (normally), therefore having family and work obligations. Other times, instead, students might not adapt to learning at a distance and need one-to-one teacher interaction to follow a course and/or learn the subject material. Distance Education does sometimes lack sufficient teacher instruction; therefore, it leaves a student needing to find answers, help, or instruction elsewhere.

Another academic challenge is when Distance Education students are not capable of setting up days and times to read, due course work, and meet deadlines for assignments or papers. Not as often, are some students who are not computer or Internet savvy and rather not deal with doing schoolwork with a computer and at a distance. Furthermore, it is sometimes challenging for Distance Education students who need to take tests find a test proctor willing to look after them during a testing session and/ or send in their test to the school. However, these challenges can be overcome, making distance education a valuable option in learning.

Conclusion

In Simple words Distance Education is an educational process and system in which all or a significant proportion of the teaching is carried out by someone or something removed in space and time from the learner. Distance Learning requires structured planning, well-designed courses special instructional techniques and methods of communication by electronic and other technology, as well as specific organizational and administrative arrangements. Distance Education has its drawbacks for learning, colleges and universities, teachers, parents, and students. When these academic challenges are tackled and solved then only the education through distance mode will be effective.

References

1. Distance Education at a Glance: http://www.uiweb.uidaho.edu/eo/dist1.html
2. Succeeding in Distance Education: http://www.cod.edu/dept/ed_tel/HowExcel.htm
3. Distance Education: Facing the Faculty Challenge:http://www.westga.edu/~distance/ojdla/summer42/bower42.html

4. *Bullen, M.* (1996). Distance Education & Technology Continuing Studies. http://www.cstudies.ubc.ca/disted

5. *Kinnaman, D.* (1995, January). The future of distance education. Technology and Learning, 15(4), p. 58.

9

Development of Self Instructional Materials For Effective Learning

Open and distance education has been accepted as an effective and viable alternative to formal education system all over the world. The term distance education is used to cover various forms of study at all levels, where the students are not in direct contact with their teachers. With the progress of new sophisticated technologies, multi-media instruction is being carried out in all open and distance education institutions. This includes print Self-Instructional Materials (SIMs), Audio and Video (broadcast and cassettes mode), Telephone, Computers, Video Disks, Teleconferencing, Teaching machines etc. However, printed material is the major medium of instruction in the most of the distance education programmes. Attempts have been made by most of our open universities to produce printed material on self-instructional format. As regards distance education institutions, the attempts are being made to develop study material from conventional format to SIM format.

Development of study material on SIM format is a challenging task and is quite different from the material meant for formal education. According to Rowntree (1986) 'the self-instructional materials must carry out all the functions a teacher would carry out in the conventional situation....guiding, motivating, intriguing, expounding, explaining, provoking, reminding, asking questions, discussing alternative answers, appraising each learners progress, giving appropriate remedial or enrichment help.... And so on'.

Instructional Strategies in Distance Education

Teaching and learning at a distance needs special instructional strategies to help students achieve their course objectives. There exist a range of instructional strategies adopted by distance education institutions.

Text Material Strategies

Specially designed printed text is a popular strategy in distance education. The printed texts are developed on the basis of the principles of designing the self-instructional materials (SIMs). The students learn from the SIMs independently, which requires skills of reading/study.

i) Broadcast Strategy: Broadcasting by using specially developed audio or video cassettes is another important strategy adopted by distance education institutions.

i) On-line Strategy: This is the latest strategy followed by distance education institutions using high-tech for offering education to distance students having access to high-tech at their home of at designated places.

Components of SIMs: SIM consist of two broad components that serve specific pedagogic functions. These components adhere to the principles of effective learning.

The components are:

A) Active Learning: Thinking, Writing, Doing

B) Access Devices: Title, Structure of the Unit, Objectives, Illustrations, Summary, Glossary

Designing of SIMs (Distinctive Features of SIM)

Individual Learning, Self-pacing learning ,Private learning, Available at any place, Available to any number, Standardised content, Expert content, Updateable content Structured teaching, Active learning, Frequent feedback ,Explicit objectives, Individualised tutoring.

Pre-requisites for Course Writers/Designers

Familiarity with the system, Familiarity with the target group, Familiarity with syllabus, Familiarity with theories of learning, Effective communication.

Process of Designing SIMs

Need assessment, Defining objectives, Identifying and organizing the content, Analysing resources and constraints, Selection of appropriate methods, media and activities, writing lessons/units, Evaluation.

Preparation of SIM Unit

i) Arranging topics/concept mapping
ii) a) concept i.e. perceived regularity in events
iii) b) proposition i.e. linking words between concepts
iv) c) Hierarchical structure in the way events take place.
v) Preparing unit structure

- X Unit title ,

Unit Structure,

- X.0 Introduction
- X.1 Objectives,
- X.2 (Main topic 1),
- x.2.1 ...Sub-topic 1,
- x.2.2 ...Sub-topic 2,
    - x.2.n ...Sub-topic n,

- X.3 (Main topic 2), X.n (Main topic n) X.(n+1) Summary,
    - X. (n+2) Answers to Check the progress

vi) Writing the unit

- Beginning of the unit : Unit structure, Introduction of the Unit, Objectives
- Main body of the unit: Logical arrangement of learning points, Ordering of content, Personalized style, Language, Illustrations, Assessment
- Ending of the unit: Summary, Glossary, References and suggested readings, Answer to self-check Questions.

SIMs is the specially designed and developed instructional materials to meet the needs, interests and problems of distance learners. In these materials the distance teacher performs, through media and technology, the roles and functions of a classroom teacher who does them mostly through oral medium. In these materials the instruction is well programmed with a view to providing an opportunity to the learners to effectively participative, get immediate feedback and gain success experiences. The SIMs enables the learners to learn according to their own pace of learning, interest, ability and convenience with minimum assistance from the distance teacher/ instructor/institution.

The SIMs is essential for distance education because they address many problems that may arise in the process of isolate learning of individual distance learners.

References

1. Teaching Machines and Self-Instructional Materials- A.A.Lumsdaine
2. Development of Evaluation Criteria for Self-Instructional Materials for Distance Education- Anil Kumar-Journal of Distance Education
3. Lewis,R. (1981): How to Write Self-study Material, Council for Educational Technology, London.

10

Mass Media and Their Educational Impact of Distance Learners

Introduction

Radio and Television are the most effective and popular mass media of communication. These two media reach out even to the illiterate masses; they are highly useful in our efforts to provide non-formal education. They are capable of utilizing the services of expert-teachers and making quality education available to millions of people at their 'drawing hall'. However they provide one-way communication only and hence cannot completely replace teachers in the true communicative process. Even with this limitation, it still plays a significant role in educating the masses through non-formal education. Radio and television broadcasts are systematically planned and organized so that they attract the listeners / viewers and stimulate them to respond in the desired way. This truth is illustrated by the increasing volume of commercial advertisements and sponsorship Programmes for business promotion.

Television can bring the events in the external world, life-like to the classroom. Sometimes we may not be able to see accurately all the details so clearly in our direct experience as we can view through the television Programmes. The total solar eclipse which occurred recently, live broadcast of cricket matches etc.). Television Programmes may be of direct relaying of films, video-tapes, projected. This facility makes it superior to films, video-tapes, projected slides, still- pictures, VCDs etc. as a teaching skills, problem- solving capacity, business entrepreneurship, marketing expertise, health care etc. among the people.

Educational Television

Television transmission has the added advantage of the all-important visual experience which is made more dynamic and meaningful by the movement and sound associated with the visual experience. The makes the television a powerful agency of communication.

This powerful mass-media of communication was first utilized in 1960 to Telecast Educational Programmes for school children in Delhi. In this, instructions in Maths, Science and English were accorded a prime place.

In 1975-76 Educational Programmes were arranged for rural children in Andhra Pradesh, Karnataka, Madhya Pradesh, Orissa and Rajasthan using the satellite ATS-F provided by the U.S.A.2 teachers from each of the 400 rural schools covered in this project received training.

In 1986,the Satellite INSAT-IB was launched by the Indian government. The Central Institute of Educational Technology situated at Delhi, utilized the services of INSAT-IB to telecast educational Programmes in the elementary school subjects (Particularly science and social studies) for 11/2 hours daily in the morning, on all days except Sunday.

Instructional Television Programme

Many telecasts, in addition to Programmes exclusively for schools, can be considered educational in a general way and viewed by pupils with advantage. Hence 'Educational Television' (ETV) includes Programmes whose primary interest is to educate rather than entertain. ETV generally includes instructional television and non-commercialized television Programmes.

'Instructional television' (ITV), on the other hand includes Programmes related directly to organized Programme of formal instruction and is directed to individual viewers who come under non-formal education Programme. In all these cases, suitable follow-up work by the teacher is essential to consolidate the gain of knowledge.

Since the Programmes are announced earlier, the institutions can prepare the pupils in advance to view and listen to telecast. TV provides multimedia learning experience.

Viewing the Television Programme

Assuring effective viewing conditions as well as learner involvement and response are essential to get the most out of ETV.TV viewing should not be done in total darkness; vision will be impaired particularly in the case of children. The viewer should not be at a distance of less than six times the diagonal of the screen.

Pupils after viewing a particular Programme should be involved in follow-up activities like written tests, home assignments, related project work etc. The teacher's responsibilities in ETV include arranging suitable physical climate in the classroom, activities during the Programme and follow up activities after the Television.

Educational Television and TV can be used in three basic ways:

1. **Total TV Teaching:** TV is the only teacher in the classroom. In a way, the Programme replaces the teacher. Such use of TV is seen in the education of children in very remote areas not covered by schools.

2. **TV as a Complementary Basic Resource:**In this type, TV acts as a basis for the total teacher process. It complements other instruction media.

3. **TV as a Supplementary Environment:** TV brings the latest information to a topic of classroom discussion.

Educational Television and Radio

The stations of the All India Radio broadcast educational Programmes for primary school–children in sixteen regional languages, including Hindi. These Programmes are broadcast for 15 to 20 minutes on three to five working days in a week for general awareness. The broadcasts for secondary school students are based on the prescribed syllabus and are relayed for 15 to 20 minutes on all school working days in a week. Adult education Programmes are also covered by radio broadcast of 15 minutes duration a week by about 14 All India Radio stations.

The National Council of Educational Research and Training (NCERT), New Delhi, Has developed a number of Programmes on school education. The national TV network through INSAT-IB telecasts these school education Programmes for students in the age-group of 6-8 years and 9-11 years daily in the morning for 3 hours and 45 minutes on about 220 school days in five regional languages, namely, Hindi, Gujarati, Marathi, Oriya and Telugu. These are telecast from Monday to Friday for primary school – teachers on Saturday.

The UGC develops enrichment Programmes in English on higher education. These Programmes are telecast on the national television network for one hour followed by a repeat telecast the same day on five days a week through the "countrywide classroom Programmes". Some imported Programmes are also telecast on the national TV network. Adult education Programmes in regional languages are also telecast by some regional television centers.

IGNOU has developed some video and audio programmes to supplement the print material for its courses, and since 1991 these programmes are being telecast on the national TV network for half an hour in the mornings, there days a week.

Educational Value of TV

1. Communication by TV is effective because it can bring very good demonstrations and audio visual materials to the classroom.
2. TV can bring the world to the home and to the classroom.
3. TV facilitates a school or college to share its best teachers rather than rationing them.
4. It helps to provide education to children even in places where there are no schools or teaches such as far off hilly places.
5. TV can save the time and effort of the student and teacher.
6. The concrete nature of TV makes some programmes understandable appealing to a wide variety of age and educational levels of people.
7. TV can be both instructive and enjoyable.

Instructional Television Programmes tend to bring into the classroom learning experiences that local teacher cannot arrange. These include costly demonstrations complicated experiments, visual excursions to far places and current events Such Programmes carefully produced and involving all kinds of interrelated learning experiences produce good results.

Limitations of TV

1. TV is a one-way communication. It does not stop to answer questions. It does not permit class discussion.
2. There is on personal contact with the teacher. The programmes do not adjust well to individual differences.

3. TV encourages a passive form of learning rather than an active seeking. It cannot provide for individual and group activities. It does not provide for laboratory experience.
4. It is very difficult to adjust the time-table of the school to fit with the instructional programmes telecast.
5. Teacher may feel they are slighted and their importance get eroded
6. If the teachers do not prepare the pupils well before viewing the television programmes, the programmes prepared with huge cost and labour may prove to be ineffective.
7. Students seated at the back benches may not be able to see the TV screen well. To eliminate this 4 or 5 T.V. sets are to be erected at vantage points in the classroom in order to be quite effective.
8. Producing effective instructional television programmes are difficult, expensive, cumbersome and requires lot of expertise.

Conclusion

Television is a powerful mass-media of communication to promote literacy among the people, develop proper attitudes and interests in them enabling to function effectively in today's world of science and technology. By using TV excessively for recreation alone, we are under- utilizing its. Versatile capacity. In many of the developed countries separate channels are allotted exclusively for telecasting educational programmesIn Tamilnadu TV Programme like "Manaimatchi" (Uû]Uôh£), "VayalumVazhvum" (YVÛmYôrÜm), "VazhkaiKalvi" (YôrdûLLp®), "UzhaypavarUlagam" (EûZlTYoEXLm), "AriviyalAyiram" (A±®VpA«Wm), "NoolVimarsanam" (èp-®UoN]m), "Care for physical health" (EPpSXmúTÔúYôm), etc. are telecast, catering to the needs and interests of various sections of the society.For example in the Programme " VayalumVazhvm", topics like 'New Agricultural practices', 'Pest control', 'Manuring', "Water Management", "Genetically Modified seeds", etc. are discussed which prove to be highly beneficial and educative for farmers of Tamilnadu. Effective utilization of ETV/ TV Programmes will depend upon proper maintenance of equipment as well as on the provision of good viewing and listening facilities in schools and teacher have to be trained in the provision of such conditions. Further, class teacher's involvement ultimately determines how much pupils learn from a TV Programme.

11

Factors Affecting Quality in Distance Education

Introduction

According to Rig vedha"Education is that which makes a man self-reliant and self-less. Swami Vivekananda remarked " Education is the manifestation of divine perfection already existing in man" He further said " we want that education by which character is formed, strength of mind is increased , the intellect is expanded and by which one can stand on one's own feet"

Till the 19thcentury, in many parts of the world including the Western countries, education was a rare privilege enjoyed by the ruling elites, landlords, nobles and the rich. That is to say, one's education, employment and social status were largely determined by birth and aristocracy. After the industrial revolution, when occupations multiplied and economic renaissance took place, 'merit and talent' were recognized and given their due place. Thus 'meritocrasy' replaced 'aristocracy' in the selection of people for education and employment.

Aims of education

The researcher desires to classify the aims of education into a few categories.

Individual aim of education

Education which is directed in this direction has a magnificent impact and will have an increasing all round and natural development of the individual.

Social aim of education

The state is the embodiment of reason, justice and morality and the individual is inferior to it in all respects. The state or society alone is the reality and the individual is only "a throb in the social pulse" It has a mission and destiny to fulfil which is the good and greater glory of itself.

Vocational aim of education

"Bread and Butter aim"/"Blue Jackal aim"/White collar aim"

Education should have a Utilitarian aim and enable the physical and help to make both ends meet in order to live happily.

Liberal or knowledge aim of education

According to Plato, "That education is Illiberal which aims at the acquisition of wealth or bodily strength apart from intelligence and justice. Illiberal education is not worthy to be called education at all"

Harmonious aim of education

It is to produce a well-balanced personality. It is the harmonious cultivation of the Physical, intellectual, aesthetic, spiritual sides of Human nature.

Moral or Character building aim

According to Sri.Radhakrishnan, the truth of the whole world including India is due to the fact that education has become a mere intellectual exercise and not the acquisition of moral and spiritual value.

Cultural Aim of education

In its Broader sense Culture is the acquaintance with the best that has been thought and said in the world since its creation somewhere in the hoary past. This education for culture aims at the cultivation and propagation of such knowledge and habits of thought which will beautify human personality and add grace to human life. As Mathew Arnold puts it, "The best that has been thought and known is culture"

Complete living aim of education

Herbert Spencer says "To prepare us for complete living is the function which education is to discharge and the important aim of changing any educational cause is to judge into what degree it discharges its function.

Spiritual aim of education

Education should aim at the maximum development of the spiritual potentialities of man. The present ills of the world, like hatred, selfish motives, chaos and disorder will have to vanish into thin air. Education on spiritual lines will replace love in the place of hatred ,sacrifice in the place of selfishness, non- violence in the place of violence, order and peace in the place of disorder and bring contentment in the world by cultivating Faith in TRUTH, **BEAUTY AND GOODNESS**

Democratic aim of education

Based on the principle of equal freedom and equal rights for all regardless of race, religion, sex, occupation or economic status, it is the way of living without any discrepancy in economic or even social aspects. It helps to enhance co-operation, tolerance, mutual respect, fellow-feeling and fair-play. Though social status, in the earlier century still remained largely 'ascribed' (determined by one's birth) a definite change was visible in different societies of the 20thcentury, to go for 'acquired statuses (earned through educational and economic status)

Meaning of "Quality" In Education

The word" quality" means high level of attainment, which is nothing but a multiple dimension of character. Human abilities are many like verbal ability, numerical ability, ability to imitate creativity, imagination, rapidity in execution, accuracy etc., Education which helps towards attaining mastery in those human abilities which are relevant and significant is referred to as "Quality Education" which is understood in terms of each of the following independently and in integration with each other.

a) Minimum level of attainment/mastery, fixed for pupils knowledge, attitude and skills.

b) Nature of the learning materials provided and the instructional techniques adopted for students' learning, which are to be evaluated in terms of 'appropriateness ' and 'adequacy'

c) How far does the output commensurate to the input involved?

Factors Affecting Quality In Education

I. Stimulating Environment: Environment is a formative factor; a good and congenial environment elevates the learner's aptitude, which a bad one debases. Therefore, children should be provided a good environment with all the physical facilities.

II. Ample supply of quality teachers: The number of learners per teacher should not be more than the prescribed ratio. If there is an increase, then the teacher can only instructor drill but cannot educate. Large classes can mean ineffective methods of teaching. Hence the student - teacher ratio should be adequate.

III. Appointing quality teachers:

No education is better than the level of its teachers. According to Erasmus, the teacher has three functions-PLACET(he pleases) DOCET(he teaches or instructs) MOVET (he moves or inspires) Almost any teacher can please and even up to a certain level instruct, But only GOOD TEACHERS CAN INSPIRE. If education today is keeping abreast with the modern knowledge, encourages children to experiment, feel, explore, learn for themselves and humanize knowledge, then such teachers can be called PEOPLE OF SUPERB QUALITY.

Ways & Means of Providing Quality Education

I. Student's self-learning activities should be more than the traditional class room instruction.

II. Auto-education (self-learning mode) and "own-time "education (distance mode, open education programmes) of the non-formal system should be given importance and expanded on a large scale.

III. A system of education that suits the needs of not only today's world but also of the future should be provided.

IV. The content methodology should be periodically updated, so as to include the latest trends in the development of Science, Arts and Technology.

V. Children should be taught to think individually, with a wider horizon with a persistent habit of reasoning and enquiry.

VI. The curriculum in distance mode should build a positive self-image and self confidence in the learner.

Pros of Distance Education;

1. No age discrimination—all are levelled as playing on a large games field.
2. Re-adjusting to "CITCADIAN RHYTHM" when someone stays awake from 6 pm to late into the night, sitting in a classroom during the day never ever seems to work successfully.
3. Distance education and Online education classes offer the same material as can be found in traditional classroom settings and the instructor-student ratio is often much more appealing.
4. Costs involved in' Brick and motor' schools are much higher when fees is considered.

Conclusion

It is quite clear that the old concepts of quality in education need radical changes in the light of our society and education. We need to pause for a while to look into a different angle while measuring the quality in education.

Quality in education should therefore

a) Have the capacity to create a new social order.
b) Emphasise on Equality and Austerity
c) Abolish poverty
d) Emphasise on co-operation, self-restraint, consideration for those around
e) Be a mode of intensive pursuit of knowledge and excellence.

To put it in a nutshell, Quality in education is judged in terms of the abilities described above and the level of proficiency attained in the abilities and the relevance and utility of the abilities in the life of the learner. It can also be redefined as that which not only prepares the learner for jobs and right use of his leisure but makes him/her wise enough and adaptable enough to handle successfully the problems he/she will have to face in everyday life. Hence, Quality education must be up to-date in content as well as in methods of instruction. Our efforts should be concentrated not only on redesigning the system in terms of goals, processes, value system and content, but also on constant monitoring to improve the performance of such education which has an all important role in the improvement of quality in education.

References

1. AMREIN & BERLINER DC(2003) The Effects of high stakes testing on student motivation and Learning educational leadership 60 (5),32-38
2. ANJALI C.BONK C & HAVA N 1998 Content Analysis of Online discussion in an applied educational and Psychology course(Online) retrieved on Ap.15th 2008 http:2// Crlt.Indian.edu/publncrlt/98-2 pdf.
3. BANDURA A & WALTERS RH (1963) Social learning & Personality development NewYork.HOLT RINECHANT & WINSTON
4. CATHERINE EBER BACH, KEVIN CROWLEY; Review of Educational research vol.79 (1) pp 39-68 Proceedings of 3rd National teachers Science congress.
5. CORNOL(1992) Encouraging students to take responsibility for learning and performance, Elementary school journal vol.93 (NLP) 69-83 Sept.1992

12

Factors Affecting Quality in Distance Education

Introduction

Distance education is in the existence for more than hundred years it has changed it face from pencil paper correspondence to on line courses. This paper explores different types of distance educational problems faced to attain quality. The nature and type of the learner, faculty organisation, curriculum and its impact on quality learning are analysed.

What is Distance Education

It was during Nineteen seventies an important theory was adopted everywhere though the teacher and the student are physically separated the learning processes took place. But the success of this method mainly depends on nature of course, duration content and delivery medium. The electronic mediated and traditional distance education where quality is expected problem do exists in both methods.

Most distance education mainly depends on the course materials, assignment and project work done by the student. The use of other combinations like contact seminars, telephone, radio, television, video, computer is also used to enhance quality in distance education.

Significance of Distance Education

Country like China and India has vast population of young adult learners. It's very difficult for the institutions to offer formal method of education. The knowledge explodes so violently we need to find alternative Technology to educate the vast population. One cannot deny the role of distance education. Most Universities got life by increasing number of distance education courses in community colleges to eliminate the various problems in educating the adults like place and place of Education. The distance education differs from formal education because both the teacher and the student find themselves in multiple roles. The teacher ceases to be a source of knowledge but only the facilitator while the student participates in knowledge imparted.

Leave above the evils of technology it paves the way for personal and group interaction in distance education. The use of computer and advanced telecommunication eliminates all the hurdles in distance education and provides almost same condition faced by traditionally educated student.

Problems in Students Distribution

Distance education is student cantered learning. For quality distance education one must understand the complex nature of the students taught in distance education. Most students opt for distance education due to its high degree of flexibility and also demanding priorities at home, school and at work. The most students' characteristics may not offer good success in a distance education course or program. It is not easy to twist them towards successful contribution. We need good student motivators to participate in distance education. The Traditional student motivators may not be that effective and we need motivators knowing learners situation and need and personal characteristics. Knowing the participants he can help to decide program planning and policy formation. It is Knowles in 1980 gave the advantages and need for right student motivators.

In this complex ultra-modern situation the students stress cannot be over looked because quality distance education understands the complex nature, contextual situation, their family, work, community role, disease, personality, and learning interest. Above all socio economic condition contributes much towards quality distance education. Now a day's no single factor appears to cause non-participation. However individual student characteristic and life circumstances appear to have the greatest impact on better participation. It was wood in 1996 suggested that the 70% learners were employed while they were in distance education. Educational level prior to distance education course or programme was found to be significant, related to persistence. Their educational background ranges from more than high school to University degree. In India a survey suggests that more than 60% of the participants were employed and peruse distance education for improving educational qualification in pursue of purse and knowledge. Carr and Led with 1980 found, that house wives tend to drop out or poor participate than general participant learners. One can very well say successful quality distance education mainly depend on the participations learning environment like full time employment, stress, personal commitments his best effort in perusing distance education programme etc.

Problems Encountered By Students

More than formal education students, distance learners face more insecurity. According to Knapper 1988 the problems encounted by distance learner's fall in to different categories costs and motivator's feedback and teacher contact student support and services alienation and Isolation lack of experience and training. All these factors affect students in perusing quality distance education. The insecurities founded in personal and school related issues such as cost of study disruption in family life, lack of support from colloquies and employers. These are the major causes for drop outs and therefore lead to poor quality in distance education. The other major drawback that affects quality distance education is lack of eye to eye contact with teacher and lack of interaction. Effective reintegration measures are needed to improve quality distance education and also to reduce drop outs. Modern technological advancements in are needed to mitigate such problem so as to improve quality in distance education. Internet centres may help urban students to overcome such problems but rural students may also use mobile communication technology to overcome such problems. Thus the communication problems which are absolutely necessary for quality distance education can be solved. The lack of student planners, tutors academic centres can complicate and pull down quality in distance education. The student learners should be suitably helped to complete course and also overcome the stress. The other important problem of student learners in distance education is feeling of alienation and isolation. This is because they like larger community as they were used to it earlier. In order to overcome these problems the student learner should be provided with personal touch by conducting institutions. Many distance learning students are yet to be well versed with computer internet. When we provide such voluminous technical details the non-technical learners find it very difficult to cope with such difficulties of non-technical students should be properly mitigated with simpler and easy to follow step by step data.

Scarcity of Best Faculty in Distance Learning

In adequate faculties may affect distance learning Teaching in distance education may differ from traditional method of teaching. A good faculty need to be trained specially for distance education and they must be suitably introduced with technology like computers video component and communication software. The biggest problem with faculty is they should not be mere administrators. But must better understand their role in distance education. They must change their teaching styles to that of a mentor a tutor and a facilitator. They must be capable of meeting the distance learner's needs with face to face contact. The faculty must also adopt him to teach distance learners of different age groups. The faculty should accept distance teaching as a method and must do it with much enthusiasm. Usually senior peoples are good teachers in distance education rather than youngsters. The faculty should have flair for distance teaching and must not be forced to do so.

Organisational Problems in Distance Learning

The institutions problems in mostly structural and technological problems. The other major concern in organisation problems is availability of funds and students. With adequate technologically friendly staff organisation must find cheap technology to reduce costs in distance education. As advised by Kinnaman (1995) it is about collaboration between teacher and technology that overcomes the restrictions of time and space, enabling students to learn more in less time and with far less overhead.

One must not forget technology may be user friendly but is of no chef. Compact disc and compact disc players may replace UN inspiring study materials. But feedback from distance learners by video conferencing, 3G phones or internet is not that cheap and is not available readily for most of rural distance learners.

Problems of Distance Education Courses

It is the belief of many that distance learning is inferior to traditional courses. Even distance education courses without proper school education as foundation are not valid in some areas. Another belief is that student from formal education perform better than students from distance education. But several recent studies among both science and acts students have proved such belief are not much of significance. Though course design, delivery may be the same only institutions that student afford better placement alone are more successful condition.

Conclusion

The rapid growth of adult learners is making distance learning and was singly people choice of learning technique. Only the right study course of suitable student population proper mitigation of student problem, designing proper course materials, usage of proper motivated faculty, use of user friendly and cost effective technology and better learning institution above can overcome the problem faced in the modern world of distance education. Only them quality distance education will be possible otherwise it remain as more dream. This paper explores the various factors affecting distance learning in adults and elders. Emerging student population, lack of experienced faculty, technological problems, curriculum development, cost effective, interactive up gradable technology are the present problems in the mammoth task of distance adult lifelong learning.

13

Teacher Education Through Distance Education: A Perspective

Education is dynamic nature and it passes through different stages of development. Education is the rare asset of an Individual, the possession of which makes one qualitatively different from those who are deprived of it Distance Education satiates the hunger of the younger and elder alike for more education and skill development. Distance Education is becoming popular day by day all over the world. The following points serve as the basis of distance education.

1. Education is a lifelong process
2. One can learn at stage of development
3. "Education or all" irrespective of barriers of distance, age, time and place.
4. Meeting the psychological, intellectual , social and emotional needs of learners
5. Improvement of standard of living
6. Equity and equality in Education.

Distance Education in Teacher Education

The world needs better teachers and more teachers to give Education to All. Distance Education helps to raise the skill of the existing teachers. The knowledge and skills of the teachers are no longer fixed and familiar targets but moving ones. Teachers, therefore need more opportunities than even before to go on learning throughout their careers. One of the ways of strengthening the teaching profession is to use distance education.

Distance Education provides, a route to initial qualification for significant number of teachers, both new entrants to teaching and experienced unqualified teachers. Continuing professional development enables teacher to extend existing knowledge and skills and develop new ones. Initial teacher education is no longer seen enough, distance education is therefore also being used to raise the skills, deepen the understanding and extend the knowledge o teachers.

Distance Education has also been useful for teacher's career development. As they seek promotion, or aim for the next qualification level, or aspire to become a head master/ headmistress or work in a college of education or an administrator, teachers need to acquire new skills.

Some Issues of Open and Distance Learning in Teacher Education

The following are some of the areas where if proper attention is paid, the quality of the Distance Teacher Education can be enhanced.

Quality of the study materials and its content

In Distance Teacher Education, learners mainly depend on the study materials given by the universities and corresponding institutions. The course content should, be intermittently linked to the learning objectives and the learner's characteristics knowledge, skills and experience. The content provided should be accurate and relevant to the needs o the learners and the society in general.

Contact classes

Many of the universities are conducting contact classes for the benefit of the student's teachers. These seminars and workshops aimed at enhancing the competencies, writing and communication skills of them. These classes should be necessarily handled by experts chosen from the academic world for their expertise and outstanding teaching ability. They should cover a wide range of important subjects to clear the difficulties of the student teachers Group work activities should be given, in contact classes to focus specific thrust on practical aspects. The learners are mainly relying on the classes conducted by the institutions.

Use of ICT

In terms of instructional methods, distance education in advanced countries have seen four generations (Taylor, 1998)

1. The Correspondence Model: Printed material by post.
2. The Multi-media Model: Print, Audiotape, Videotape, Computer – Based Learning, Interactive Video.
3. The Tele-learning Model : Audio Teleconferencing, Video Conferencing
4. The Flexible Learning Model: Interactive Multimedia, Internet Based Access, Computer Mediated Communication.

Most of the universities in our country are still in the first generation level. Very few universities have made modest beginning with the third and fourth generation level. So all the universities should use, ICT instructional methods so that the learners can acquire deeper understanding of the subject.

Parity between the Curriculum of Regular Programme and Distance Education

There should be a co-ordination in the distance education programmes and regular programmes regarding curriculum, syllabus, and its evaluation. This facilitates the regular and distant learners on par with their subject knowledge and content. In ensures and encourages the students to study further and move upwards in the ladder of education and employment.

Constructive feed back

The distance education learners may be asked to give constructive feedback on the course content, contact classes, and its utility for them. Feedback thus collected could be used to review the programmes. The suggestions will certainly help to keep the pace of the programme and its relevance.

Conclusion

Teacher Education in distance mode may reach large group of teachers and have profound impact on the development of National Education systems. Distance education offers life ling learning potential for teachers and will play a significant part in educating students and teachers around the world. The goals of teacher education in distance education and education under face to face mode are not different. The international goals of creating a learning society, where the women and all the disadvantaged are empowered, a society free of hunger, a society with sustainable development, etc. cannot be created by the efforts of formal sector under face to face mode alone. A vibrant Open and Distance Learning mode of Teacher Education Programme is a must for achieving these lofty goals of Education.

References

1. Agrawal,A.K.(2005) Development of Education System in India. Anmol Publications Pvt.Ltd., New Delhi.
2. Hegde,G.(2008) Accreditation of Open and Distance Learning in Indian Contexts: Some Methodological Issues, ***University News***, 46(36) September 08-14.2008.

3. Kratermik,R.(2001)Teacher Education through Distance Learning Summary of Case Studies Technology, curriculum, Education Cost, UNESCO, France.

4. More,M.M. and Trait,A.(2002) Open and Distance Learning Trends, Policy and Strategy Considers UNESCO, France.

5. Verma,R.(2007) Status of Distance Education in Indian, ***University News,*** 45(41),October 08-14.

14

F-learning - A New Approach to Distance Education

Introduction

Distance education is one of the most dramatic of recent technology-based innovations in education. Many educators are making grand claims about how distance education is likely to change education and training. Certainly, the concept of distance education is exciting, and recent hardware and software innovations are making telecommunications systems more available, easier to use, and less costly. Distance education has begun to enter the mainstream.

Distance Education Today and Tomorrow

Distance educators are being confronted by two conflicting pressures. First, *students do not really want to learn at a distance.* They prefer to meet with the learning group and the instructor in the lecture hall, the classroom, the seminar room, or the laboratory.

Second, *students are increasingly demanding to be allowed to learn at a distance.* They want to be able to supplement, and even replace conventional learning experiences with distance education experiences. This is because there are many other considerations than personal preferences that motivate learners, especially about where and when they learn.

These opposing forces pose a dilemma for the educational community. Should resources be dedicated to improving the traditional educational infrastructure of buildings, classrooms, laboratories, and offices, or should resources be used to develop modern and sophisticated telecommunications systems.

Technology in Distance Education

Because of advances in technology, effective educational experiences can be provided for learners, no matter where they are located. In other words, technologies are now available to develop cost-effective distance education systems.

The practice of distance education has dramatically changed in the last five years. Traditional approaches to distance education based on the delivery of print and linear media technologies are no longer as relevant to the field as it is practiced. As a matter of fact, a redefinition of the distance education has occurred.

Distance education is now often defined as: “institution-based, formal education where the learning group is separated geographically, and where interactive telecommunications systems are used to connect learners, resources, and instructors.”

Flexible Learning

Flexible Learning is a set of educational philosophies and systems, concerned with providing learners with increased choice, convenience, and personalisation to suit the learner. In particular, flexible learning provides learners with choices about where, when, and how learning occurs. Sometimes also referred to as personalised learning.

Flexible learning approaches are often designed using a full range of teaching and learning theories, philosophies and methods to provide students with opportunities to access information and expertise, contribute ideas and opinions, and correspond with other learners and mentors. This may occur through the use of internet-based tools such as Virtual Learning Environments (VLEs) or Learning Management Systems (LMSes), discussion boards or chat rooms; and may be designed as a "blended" approach, with content available electronically and remotely, as well as "face-to-face" classroom tutorials and lectures.

While the majority of flexible learning programs have taken advantage of computer-based systems ("E-learning"), the rapidly increase in the processing power and popularity of mobile digital devices has recently caused considerable interest in mobile learning - the use of mobile devices such as mobile phones, iPods, and Personal Digital Assistants (PDAs) to increase the mobility of learners and correspondingly enhance the flexibility of their learning.

Flexible Learning As A Concept

Flexible learning is commonly used with various other terms including flexible delivery, open learning, resource based learning, distance learning, independent learning and self-managed learning. Conceptually, flexible learning is generally sited within the open learning field: " the concept of open education is ill defined but has to do with matters relating to access, freedom from constraints of time and place, means, structure, dialogue and the presence of support services. Openness in terms of means would imply the presence of choice between distance and contiguous modes as well as choice between specific media. Most of these features relate to educational policy and philosophy rather than the modality of teaching"

Flexible learning began to be used as a term in the UK in the early 1980's. Wade defines flexible learning as "an approach to education which provides learners with the opportunity to take greater responsibility for their learning and to be engaged in learning activities and opportunities that meet their own individual needs".

Hudson defines flexible learning as "essentially learner cantered learning... aimed at improving access, giving learners control and choice over what and how they learn, helping them to take responsibility for their learning and providing support appropriate to the individual's needs"

Flexible Learning Approach

In its essence, flexible learning is about greater choice for learners. This includes choices in when, where and how learning occurs. Adopting a flexible learning approach doesn't mean changing everything about our approach to teaching and learning. Many current practices can be part of a flexible approach. Educational approaches and strategies that contribute to flexible learning include:

1. Workplace training
2. Community classes
3. Study centres
4. Recognition of Prior Learning
5. Alternative learning pathways to various levels of accreditation
6. Self-paced and self-access study
7. Work-based projects
8. Mentored learning
9. Teleconferencing
10. Video conferencing
11. Using a range of learning activities (role play, simulation, reading, listening, presentations, group work, discussion, out-of-class projects etc)
12. Student support services
13. Using a range of resource types (print-based, web-based, multi-media)

Flexible learning can be viewed as an incentive to reflect on teaching and learning environments, and develop new ways to engage with students. Flexible learning is not a goal in itself; the goal is to improve the learning experience and the learning outcomes. Flexible learning is a method by which educational goals can be achieved. This means that the decision to implement particular flexible learning strategies should be informed by educational values and goals and by specific educational contexts.

Conclusion

Separation of the student and the teacher is a fundamental characteristic of distance education. Increasingly, educators are using technology to increase the access of the distant learner to the local classroom, and to make the experience of the remote student comparable to the experience of the local learner. Distance education is a dramatic idea. It may change, even restructure, education, but only if it is possible to make the experience of the distant learner as complete, satisfying, and acceptable as the experience of the local learner.

F-learning enhances the learning experience by expanding the boundaries of the classroom. Distance education through flexible learning approach is an exciting emerging field.

References

1. http://flexways.flexiblelearning.net.au/aboutfl/whatisfl.asp
2. http://www.col.org/pcf3/papers/PDFs/Gerbic_Philippa.pdf
3. http://en.wikipedia.org/wiki/Flexible_learning
4. http://www.col.org/pcf3/papers/PDFs/Gerbic_Philippa.pdf
5. http://fie-conference.org/fie96/papers/223.pdf

15

Students Learning Style and Design of Distance Education

Distance education is emerging as a viable and vital force in educational delivery system in recent years, especially in higher education. Much of the growth comes from a rapidly growing demand for educational opportunities directed toward and designed for some specific target groups (Garrison, 1986; 1987; Gaspar & Thompson, 1995). Just as Amundsen and Bernard (1989) pointed out, "...the definitive characteristic of distance education is the separation between 'teacher' and learner and among learners. In the perspective of Keegan (1986), distance education has six major features: (a) the separation of teacher and learner, (b) the role of the educational organization, (c) the place of the technological medium, (d) two-way communication, (e) the separation of learner and the learning group, and (f) industrialization. In sum, distance education establishes a system that provides learning opportunities to various groups of learners who have no access to the traditional, higher education institutions.

Learning Styles

In most situations, cognitive styles and learning styles are used interchangeably. Generally, cognitive styles are more related to theoretical or academic research, while learning styles are more related to practical applications. A major difference between these two terms is the number of style elements involved. Specifically, cognitive styles are more related to a bipolar dimension while learning styles are not necessarily either/or extremes. Cognitive/learning styles measures conventionally lie somewhere between aptitude measures and personality measures.

Kolb's Experiential Learning Theory

Kolb has described four basic learning styles: accommodative, assimilative, divergent, and convergent. Incorporated within each learning style is a combination of two of the four learning modes: Concrete experiences, reflective observation, abstract conceptualization, and active experimentation. Kolb and Fry (1975) also have described four different learning environments that are most conducive for accommodating the different learning styles and learning modes. These include the affective learning environment, the symbolic learning environment, the perceptual learning environment, and the behavioral learning environment.

The Learning Styles

Assimilative Style

The assimilative learning style is characterized by the ability to reason inductively. Kolb (1984) has suggested that one of the assimilator's greatest abilities is to "create theoretical models in assimilating disparate observations into an integrated explanation" (p.78). Assimilators concern themselves with ideas and abstract concepts rather than with people and social interactions and are concerned with abstract, logical rather than practical aspects of theories. Individuals who use the assimilative style incorporate the learning modes of reflective observation and abstract conceptualization.

Accommodative Style

As opposed to the assimilative style, accommodative learners excel at accomplishing tasks by following directions, meticulously planning, and ultimately seeking new experiences (Kolb, 1984). They are characterized as being opportunistic, action driven, and risk takers. The accommodative label comes from their ability to adapt themselves to changing circumstances. Unlike assimilative learners, those who are accommodative solve problems in an intuitive trial-and-error manner rather than through careful examination of facts, and they rely heavily on other people for information rather than on their own analytic ability (Grochow, 1973; Stabell, 1973). The learning modes associated with accommodative learners include concrete experience and active experimentation.

Convergent Style

Kolb suggests that the convergent learner's greatest strength is the ability to efficiently solve problems, make decisions and apply practical ideas to solve problems. Generally, these people do well on standard conventional intelligence tests because they can organize knowledge by hypothetical deductive reasoning and thus are able to converge to one given answer (Kolb, 1976; Torrealba, 1972). Hudson (1966) suggests that people with this learning style are well adept at controlling their emotions, and prefer dealing with technical tasks and problems rather than with issues that involve interpersonal and social interactions. Convergent learners draw from the learning modesof abstract conceptualization and active experimentation.

Divergent Style

The divergent learner is best at tasks that require "imaginative ability and awareness of meaning and value" (Kolb, 1984, p. 77). Individuals with this learning style have the ability to identify concrete examples of a concept and to generate numerous qualities about this concept from many perspectives. They are then able to organize these qualities by how each quality interrelates to one another, which then provides a meaningful "gestalt" whole of the concept. They are considered "brainstormers" (p. 77), prefer to observe rather than act, are emotionally-oriented and tend to be very creative. Divergent learners prefer the learning modes of concrete experiences and reflective observation.

The Learning Modes

Concrete Experiences

The concrete experiences mode is characteristic of learners who desire plenty of opportunities for direct human interpersonal interactions. These individuals also prefer to feel and experience rather than think. Kolb describes them as intuitive decision makers, who value circumstances involving people in real world situations.

Reflective Observation

This mode focuses on the ability to understand the meaning of ideas. Individuals who are characterized by this mode value objective judgment, impartiality, and patience. They prefer abstract understanding over practical applications, and they prefer to reflect and observe rather than act on a situation.

Abstract Conceptualization

Individuals oriented toward abstract conceptualization typically attend to tasks that involve logical investigation of ideas and concepts. Unlike concrete experiences, this learning mode is characterized by a preference to depend on cognitive rather than emotional skills. Commonly, individuals who prefer this mode involve themselves with and tackle academic problems that require the ability to build general theories in order to come up with a solution. People in this mode also value rigorous idea analysis and well defined conceptual systems. Finally, this mode involves the use of "systematic planning, manipulation of abstract symbols, and quantitative analysis" (Kolb, 1984, p. 69).

Active Experimentation

"The active experimentation learning mode focuses on actively influencing people and changing situations" (Kolb, 1984, p. 69). In other words, individuals in this learning mode prefer to be involved in peer interactions that allow them to play an integral role in the decisions made in these interactions. This mode emphasizes practical applications or solutions rather than reflective understanding of a problem. People who use this mode are pragmatists and focus on doing rather than observing; they enjoy and are especially efficient at getting the "job done" (p. 69); and they truly value the ability to manipulate their environment to produce productive results.

The Learning Environments

The affective learning environment emphasizes concrete experiences so that students actually experience what it might be like to be a professional in a given field of study. Affective learning tasks include activities such as practical exercises, simulations, or field experiences. Information is usually peer oriented and delivered informally. The instructor is considered as a role model and an exemplar for the particular field of study. Activities are non-competitive, and feedback should not be comparative but personalized to the individual student's goals and needs (Kolb, 1984).

The symbolic learning environments one in which learners is involved in trying to solve problems for which there is usually a right answer or a best solution. Information is abstract and usually presented in readings, data, pictures, and lecture formats. Characteristic activities may include lecture, homework, and theory readings. The instructor is acknowledged as the expert, enforcer of rules, regulator of time, and taskmaster. This instructional format is typically didactic with a top-down, hierarchical class structure (Kolb, 1984).

According to Kolb and Fry (1975), the **perceptual learning environment**s one in which the main goal is to identify and understand relationships among concepts. Unlike activities in the symbolic environment, the perceptual environment emphasizes the process of problem solving rather than coming up with the best solution. Learners are required to collect relevant information for researching questions and are expected to attack a problem situation through different perspectives (own opinion, expert opinion and literature) by listening, observing, writing, discussing and personal pondering. In this environment, the teacher's role is to act as a facilitator of the learning process, to be non-evaluative, and to act as mirror by reflecting back student observations and comments. Learning processes may include reflective exercises such as keeping journals, writing reflective essays, or engaging in dialogue with other students. Such practices are incorporated into each class session, which emphasizes the importance of reflection on learning.

Behavioural learning environment emphasizes actively applying knowledge or skills to a practical problem. Although correct answers for activities are not necessary for success in this environment, activities should be structured so that learners gain intrinsic rewards and values. The teacher acts as a coach or guide but only when the student initiates or solicits help. Figure 1 depicts a conceptual

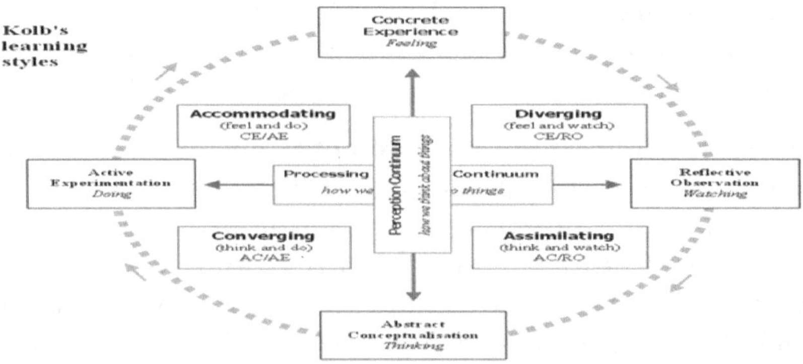

framework of the four learning styles, learning modes, and learning environments.

Design of Distance Education

Learner/teaching styles are one of the several important factors to be considered by the designers and teachers of the distance education classes (Kieran-Greenbush, 1993). However, not much research has been done regarding the adaptation of distance education to students' learning styles. Suggestions for the adaptation of the design and delivery of distance education will be proposed below in terms of four major instructional stages:

Learner Analysis The teacher should use appropriate cognitive style instruments to measure and identify the student's cognitive styles either before the start of the first class or in the first class. The teacher should be sure to know the students' preferred cognitive styles. All these will become the basis for the teacher to prepare for the distance education classes.

Matching Cognitive style and teaching methods

After identifying students' cognitive styles, the teacher should make a full preparation for the match between cognitive styles and instructional contents, methods, and styles. These include: (a) what kind of instructional materials to teach, (b) what kind of learning environments to provide, (c) what kind of teaching methods and styles to use, such as the appropriate use of tapes, diagrams, etc., (d) what kind of formal instruction and informal activities to plan, and (e) what kind of evaluation techniques to use. In order to effectively match the teaching styles with the students' cognitive styles, the teacher should take the following considerations. This part involves two major aspects.

1. Matching the instructional materials with cognitive styles
2. Matching the teaching styles with cognitive styles

Learning Environment Construction

To accommodate all types of learning styles, the course designer should consider how to incorporate each learning environment suggested by Kolb and Fry (1975) Learning environment should be constructed and it should be match and support with the various learning styles and their associated modes.

Evaluation Administration

The administration of evaluation in distance education includes two major aspects. One is assessment; the other is feedback about assessment.

1. Assessment: Assessment is used to measure what and how the students have learned in the distance education classes.

2. Feedback: The teacher should provide appropriate timely feedback regarding the results of the above assessment outcomes, such as exams, assignments, projects, and papers. In addition, the feedback should be primarily positive and encouraging.

Conclusion

The instructional adaptation and design of distance education to the students' cognitive styles appear more important than traditional classroom education. It is sometimes difficult for instructors to recognize the importance of consideration of individual student needs. If more workshops are conducted faculty- wise to train the faculty for preparation of material according to the students learning style, it will be useful to the learner.

Bibliography

1. Amundsen, C. L., & Bernard, R. M. (1989). Institutional support for peer contact in distance education: An empirical investigation. Distance Education, 10 (1), 7-27.
2. Garrison, D. R. (1986). The role of technology. In R. G. Brockett

(Ed.), Continuing education in the year 2000 (pp.41-54). San Francisco: Jossey Bass.

3. Garrison, D. R. (1987). The role of technology in continuing education. New Directions for Continuing Education, 36, 41-53.
4. Gaspar, R. F., & Thompson, T. D. (1995). Current trends in distance education. Journal of Interactive Instruction Development, 8 (2), 21-27.
5. Grochow, J. (1973). Cognitive style as a factor in the design of interactive decision-support systems. Unpublished master's thesis, Massachusetts Institute of Technology, Cambridge, Massachusetts, United States.
6. Hudson, L. (1966). Contrary imaginations. Middlesex, England: Penguin Books. Jones, C., Richard, C., &Mokhtar, K. (2003). Is students' learning styles discipline specific? Community College Journal of Research and Practice, 27(5), 363-375
7. Keegan, D. (1986). The foundations of distance education. Dover, New Hampshire: Croom Helm.
8. Kolb, D. A. (1976). Learning-Style Inventory, Boston, MA: McBer and Company.
9. Kolb, D. A. (1984). Experiential learning: Experience as the source of learning and development, Upper Saddle River, New Jersey: Prentice Hall.
10. Kolb, D. A., & Fry, R. E. (1975). Toward an applied theory of experiential learning, In C.Cooper, (Ed), Theories of group processes. London: Wiley Press.
11. Stabell, C. (1973). The impact of a conversational computer system on human problemsolvingbehavior. Unpublished master's thesis, Massachusetts Institute of Technology, Cambridge, Massachusetts, United States.
12. Torrealba, D. (1972). Convergent and divergent learning styles. Unpublished master's thesis, Massachusetts Institute of Technology, Cambridge, Massachusetts, United States.

16

Instructional Development For Distance Education

Introduction

Distance education refers to being able to study or take up a course without being present physically for the course but being able to take it up through any other medium. Instructional development provides a process and framework for systematically planning, developing and adapting instruction based on identifiable learner needs and content requirements.

Although instructional development models and processes abound, the majority follow the same basic stages of design, development, evaluation and revision. While it is possible, even appropriate on occasion, to shorten the instructional development process, it should be done only after considering the needs of the learner, the requirements of the content and the constraints facing both teacher and students.

The need for instructional development

The instructional development is essential in distance education, where the instructor and students may share limited common background and typically have minimal face-to-face contact. The four stages of instructional development processes are Design, Development, Revision and Evaluation.

The instructional development process

Design

- Determine need-Analyze audience-Establish goals.

Development

- Develop and implement revision plan-create content outline.

Revision

- Review existing materials.
- Organize and develop content.
- Select/develop materials and delivery methods.

Evaluation

- Review goals and objectives.
- Develop evaluation strategy.
- Collect and analyse data.

The design stage

Determine the need for instruction

To begin, determine the need for instruction by considering what external data verify the need, what factors led to the instructional need and what past experiences indicate that the instruction being planned can effectively meet this need.

Analyze your audience

To better understand the distant learners and their needs, consider their ages, cultural backgrounds, past experiences, interests and education levels. Assess their familiarity with the various instructional methods and delivery systems being considered; determine how they will apply the knowledge gained in the course and note whether the class will consist of a broad mix of students or discrete subgroups with different characteristics (eg. urban/rural undergraduate/ graduate). When possible, the instructor should visit distant sites and interview prospective students, both individually and in small groups. This personalized attention will also show students that the instructor is more than an anonymous presence, linked by electronic technology. Colleagues who have worked with the target population can also offer advice.

Establish instructional goals/objectives

Based on the nature of the problem as well as student needs and characteristics, establish instructional goals and objectives. Goals are broad statements of instructional intent, while objectives are specific steps leading to goal attainment.

Create a content outline

Based on the instructional problems, the audience analysis, instructional goals and objectives and an understanding of the desired course content, create an outline of the content to be covered.

Review existing materials

Next the instructor should review existing materials. Instructional material should not be used solely because they are readily available. This is especially true if pre-packed materials, such as tele-courses, as being considered. Whereas many pre-packed instructional tools are developed and marketed to reach students with similar backgrounds and expenses, they may have little relevance of distant learners who come to the course with widely varied and non-traditional experiential backgrounds. If pre-packaged instructional materials are to be used, consider developing "wrap around" introductions, conclusions and summaries that specifically relate the learning materials to the instructional context of the distant student.

Organize and develop content

Perhaps the greatest challenge facing the distant educator is creating student – relevant examples. The best examples are "transparent" allowing the learners to focus on the content being presented. If examples are irrelevant learning is impeded. This is a special challenge in rural and multicultural settings where the teacher's realm of experience and content examples may be foreign to distant learners. To address this problem, discuss potential content examples with a sampling of the target audience.

Select/develop materials and methods

The development of instructional materials and selection of delivery methods will often require integrating print, voice, video and data technology in concert with face-to-face communication. The challenge here is to integrate delivery components, based on identifiable learner needs, content requirements and technical constraints.

The evaluation stage

Review goals and objectives

One purpose of evaluation is to determine if the instructional methods and materials are accomplishing the established goals and objectives. Implementation of instruction represents the first real test of what has been developed.

Develop and evaluation strategy: plan how and when to evaluate the effectiveness of the instruction.

Formative evaluation can be used to revise instruction as the course is being developed and implemented.

Summative evaluation in conducted after instruction is completed and provides a data base for course revision and future planning. Within the context of formative and summative evaluation, data are collected through quantitative and qualitative methods.

Quantitative evaluation relies on a breadth of response and is patterned after experimental research focused on the collection and manipulation of statistically relevant quantities of data.

Qualitative evaluation focuses on a depth of response, using more subjective methods such as interviews and observation to query a smaller number of respondents in greater depth.

Collect and analyze evaluation data

Following implementation of your course/ materials, collect the evaluation data. Careful analysis of these results will identify gaps or weaknesses in the instructional process. It is equally important to identify strengths and successes.

The revision stage

There is room for improvement in even the most carefully developed distance delivered course and the need for revision should be anticipated. In fact, there will likely be more confidence in a course that has been significantly revised that in one considered flawless the first time through.

Revision plans typically are a direct result of the evaluation process in tandem with feedback from colleagues and content specialists. The best source of revision ideas may be the instructor's own reflection on course strengths and weaknesses. For this reason, revision should be planned as soon as possible after the course ends. Revisions should be made according to priority and significant course changes should be field – tested prior to future course scheduling to test revision ideas, contact and reconvene small groups of distant learners, content specialists and colleagues and ask them to review and critique the revision ideas being considered.

Conclusion

While it is possible, even appropriate on occasion, to shorten the instructional development process, it should be done only after considering the needs of the learner, the requirements of the content and the constraints facing both teacher and students. Adhering to sound principles of instructional development won't overcome all obstacles one encountered enrooted to developing effective distance education programs. It will, however, provide a process and procedural framework for addressing the instructional challenges that will surely arise.

References

1. Beare,P.L.(1989). The Comparative Effectiveness of Videotape, Audiotape and Telelecture in Delivering Continuing Teacher Education. American Journal of Distance Education 3(2),57-66.
2. Brooksfield,S.D. (1990). The Skilful Teacher: on Technique, Trust and Responsiveness in the Classroom. San Francisco CA: Jossey-Bass.
3. Dick, W.& Carey, L.(1990). The Systematic Design of Instruction (3rd ed.), Glenview, IL, Scott, Foreman and Company.
4. Willis, B (1993). Distance Education: A Practical Guide, Englewood Cliffs, NJ: Educational Technology Publications.
5. Flagg, B.N.(1990). Formative Evaluation for Educational Technologies. Hillsdale, NJ: Lawrence, Erlbaum Associates.

17

Distance Education For and in Inclusive Society: Initiatives And Suggestions

Introduction

The issue of educating and providing reasonable life skills to enable the individuals with disabilities has been the concern of civilized societies. While international conferences have addressed this need, Special Needs Education: Access and Quality (Salamanca, Spain1994) is a land mark commitment, it was reemphasized at the World Education Forum (Dakar, Senegal, 2000). In practice, two parallel streams, viz., special education and inclusive education for educating the disabled children have their champions placing arguments respectively. Teachers alone cannot handle this. Parents need to be aware, understand and play supportive role in early identification, reference to specialists and seeking counselling services along with training, vocation and rehabilitation. The role of supportive staff who has received specialized qualification to deal with persons with disabilities is equally important.

The gradual shift of focus from special education to integrate to inclusive requires suitable training of the parents, supportive staff and teachers. National Curriculum Framework for Teacher Education, 2009(NCTE) states that because of the inadequate competence and sensitivity of the teacher two kinds of exclusion is prevalent in schools. One is the exclusion of the child with disabilities of different kinds because the teacher does not understand their needs or what s/he can do to make learning possible for them. The second and stronger exclusion is the social exclusion that come from socially and economically deprived background (SC/ST/minority community). It further explains that the teachers who teach and manage the classroom need to be sensitized and made aware of the philosophy of inclusive education, and oriented to different kinds of adjustment that schools had to make in term of infrastructure, curriculum, teaching methods, and other school practices to relate teaching to the special needs of all children PWD act of 2005 provides for free and compulsory education up to the age of 18 years for all children with disability.

Booth, Nes, and Stromstad argue that attention must shift away from the individual students with disabilities to focus on the structures (implicit and explicit) in our schools that serve as barriers to the inclusion of all students. Some institutions have begun to find ways to begin this process. For example, some teacher education institutions are beginning to require prospective educators to receive general or traditional licensure as well as special education licensure (Nagata, 2005). This promising practice allows novice teachers to see how special education practices and theories can aid the learning of all students in JK-12 settings. When teacher educators model inclusive practices and establish programs linking traditional and special education, pre-service teachers learn vicariously about the success and necessity of acknowledging the strengths of all students. Teachers' struggles to understand the necessity of including all students in classroom practices stem, in part, from the lack of inclusive models presented when they themselves were students. Inclusion is one initiative to link the traditional and special education programs.

Significance of Distance Education

While considerable progress is made in the North America, the U.S.A., the U.K. in implementing Inclusive education, Australia ,Africa and Asia have seriously set out to pass relevant acts and implement policies with the government initiative and N.G.O.collaboration. There is lack of trained personnel for implementing IE. The DE courses take services to the doorsteps learners, and have flexibility in terms of pace, place and duration of study. Some of the foreign universities offer courses on line for different clientele.

Walden University offers Special Education Endorsement Program withM.S.in Education-Learning Disabilities (K-12) for licensed teachers who want transition into a Special Education classroom or bring their skills to the current teaching area. This practical, accelerated program combines the flexibility on line learning with hand on field experiences. In 16 months the teacher can enhance his/her skills and increase professional opportunities by fulfilling the requirements needed to teach K-12 students with special needs.

Southern New Hampshire University offers Master of Education in Curriculum & Instruction with a concentration in Special Education for practicing teachers with the desire to improve the instructional quality of their students' experience. This 18 months program explores traditional, innovative and research based approaches to support the instructional and transitional needs of children in the inclusive classroom as they progress from pre-school through high school.

Saint Joseph's University offers online Master of Science in Special Education based on Response to Intervention (RTI) designed for individuals holding Level 1early childhood, elementary teaching certification or secondary teaching certification who are seeking to become highly qualified with a certification in special education on (pre-K through 12th Grade). This degree is well suited for teachers certified in special education, who are seeking an advanced degree and general educators who are seeking a master degree based on state of the art, research- based theory and instructional practice for meeting the diverse needs of their student population.

Programs Offered By Ignou

Awareness cum training packages (MR, VI, HI and Cerebral Palsy separately) for parents and family members of children with disabilities developed in collaboration with Rehabilitation Council of India. It is a unique initiative for community workers also. Life-span perspective with particular focus on early childhood years. The packages provide knowledge, understanding and skills to foster the overall development of disabled children, offered through select NGOs across the country.

Certificate Program in Early Childhood Special education Enabling Inclusion (Cerebral Palsy) is jointly offered with the National Centre for Disability Studies. It equips learner to work as a member of an inter-disciplinary team providing early intervention to children up to 6 years of age in a variety of settings such as home- based intervention, centre-based intervention in special and/ or inclusion set ups, and community-based intervention set ups.B.Ed.(Special Education) is a collaborative program of IGNOU and RCI . It aims at the development of professionals for special and inclusive education within a broad perspective education. The program allows for specialization in one out of the areas of: hearing impairment, visual impairment and mental retardation.

Programs Offered By Madhya Pradesh Bhoj University

Under MOU signed between MPBOU and RCI, in January,2000 this university situated in Bhopal is recognized as the National Resource Centre for Special Education and Rehabilitation Programs through distance mode. The Department of Special Education (DSE) offers

- o Bachelor of Special Education through Distance Mode
- o Foundation Course on Education of Children with Disabilities
- o Post Graduate Professional Diploma in Special Education

DSE also plans to conduct: Up gradation of Skills of Personnel who is already working in the area of special education; Interdisciplinary Research and Training Programs for Rehabilitation and Empowerment of Differently Abled.

Empirical Study Comparing Traditional and Distance Instruction in Disability Courses

Larry S.Tinnerman made a comparison of traditional and distance instruction environments involving two graduate level Learning Disabilities classes, taught by him. The class sizes were 25 traditional and 22 distances respectively. Pre-test and post-test analysis showed no significant difference by t-test analysis at $p<.05$. Other items of significance using Chi-square test at $p<.05$, were centered on the following:

- Student to student communication
- Student to teacher communication
- students content understanding of communicational issues
- Impromptu and extraordinary communication
- Time spent in defining and understanding course content and expectations
- Continuity of curriculum for instructor to instructed
- Technology issues including experience and expertise of both the student and instructor
- Perceptions of distance education effectiveness.

During the course of the research, there were other factors that were observed for distance education students including: the awkwardness of communication effectively using non-verbal typed methods such as chat or discussion forum; the compatibility of various software packages; the difficulty of teacher modelling for students; the demand for the instructor to be both content expert and a technical expert.

Conclusion

Quality in conducting ***special education*** programs for teachers ***through distance mode*** needs well designed, widely available in remote places, involving committed and compassionate staff who are ***identified and motivated with recognition and suitable remuneration***.

References

1. Nan Kurz and Peter V. Paul ;Toward an Inclusive Teacher Education Program, Journal of teaching and learning, 2005, vol. 3, no. 2
2. http://itdl.org/journal/april_06/articlesus.htm
3. www.bhojvirtualuniversity.com

18

Value Considerations For the Emerging Global Learner of Distance Education

Introduction

The rapid developments in science and technology and the challenges of globalization are posing additional challenges to the education system in the country. The adverse effects of the media on the mental development and moral values of the younger generation are invading all spheres of life. Gross consumerism has distorted the outlook of persons into one of equating possessions with richness. Exploitation of natural resources is proceeding without reference to sustainability. The hiatus between the rich and the poor is getting wider. Too much emphasis on knowledge and skills in the education system needs to address the more fundamental issues of the social and moral consequences of such unbridled persuasions. In this context, there is now a growing demand to lay greater emphasis on education to inculcate, nurture and develop values, particularly among the youth of the country whether they pursue education in the regular /distance mode.

Need for Value Based Education in Higher Education

The focus should be on how to convert the youth of the country into resourceful population so that they can become the assets and not a burden on the society. The major social benefit of higher education is that it produces individuals with knowledge and skills at an academic or advanced professional level that are valuable to society. Universities should perform functions leading to important social benefits. They are,

1. Cultural transmission of values
2. Social integration
3. Promoting personal and social change
4. Establishing social networks
5. Offering extracurricular activities and social services

The NAAC lays emphasis in its accreditation frame work that the higher education institutions should strive for the five ***core values***

1. Contributing to national development
2. Fostering global competencies among students
3. Inculcating a value system among students
4. Promoting use of technology
5. Quest for excellence

Growing Demand for Distance Education

Formal means of general/vocational/professional education are not adequate. In independent India peoples' thirst for higher education and qualification improvement can be met only through distance education programs. The four pillars of education ***learning to know, learning to do, learning to live cooperatively and learning to be*** are also the guiding values of an educated society. It is a collective responsibility of all such developmental agencies to provide value inputs to the wide age groups of learners who opt for distance/ open education mode singly or in addition to regular studies. The IGNOU has taken lead in this direction, through its innovative programs under the surveillance of ODL COUNCIL without sacrificing quality.

The emerging online learner

The emerging online learner can be described as someone who has a strong academic self-concept; is competent in the use of online learning technologies, particularly communication and collaborative technologies; understands values and engages in social interaction and collaborative learning; possesses strong interpersonal and communication skills and is self-directed.

Dabbagh summarise the characteristics of the on line learner,

- Having a strong academic self-concept
- Exhibiting fluency in the use of online learning technologies
- Possessing interpersonal and communication skills
- Understanding and valuing interaction and collaborative learning
- Possessing an internal locus of control
- Exhibiting self-directed learning skills
- Exhibiting a need for affiliation

In addition to the above, a distance learner needs to possess ***social learning skills, discursive or dialogical skills, self and group evaluation skills and reflection skills.***

Virtual universities have been claimed to only reproduce the academic cognitive function of the university, and fail to reproduce most or all of the other major social benefits of universities.

Values common to regular and distance education

Academic values are values that academically trained individuals are expected to uphold in academic settings and in professional life, and that define what has been called academic integrity. They are values that directly bear on the manner in which academic work is performed, the manner in which professional interaction takes place, and the attitudes that are taken to professional work and professional interaction. Academic values include values such as honesty, objectivity, fairness, trust, collegiality, respect, accuracy, thoroughness, independence, openness, curiosity and responsibility.

Ethical issues of virtual universities

Virtual universities should consider developing policies that address the special ethical issues that emerge in educational settings that depend heavily on information and communication technologies. These policies may include some or all of the following:

1. Policies concerning digital plagiarism and academic dishonesty in online assessment

2. Policies concerning copyright and software theft

3. Policies concerning hacking. These should be supplemented by clear access guidelines to different systems and should probably distinguish malicious from no malicious hacking.

4. Policies concerning the proper use of computer resources of the university.

5. Policies concerning online anonymity and pseudo anonymity, online harassment and hate speech, which should at the same time, not impose unacceptable limits on free speech.

6. Privacy policies for personal information stored in databases and for online privacy.

Taking values seriously in the development of virtual university programs requires placing these values at the core of every structure and procedure that is developed or used. This requires that such values are taken into account throughout the development of institutional models, curricula, administrative policies, software programs, etc., and that they function as a continuous touchstone as well as a source of inspiration for their development and use of such structures.

For values to function as such, they must be reflected upon, and be discussed. Reflection on and discussion of values should therefore be considered an integral part of the development of virtual university programs, and should indeed be a recurring activity within universities themselves.

Education for tomorrows' global citizen

1. Education in the future should reflect and incorporate principles of " global citizenship education; emphasizing universal concepts
2. Value formations should be an integral part incorporated in every subject
3. Education in the future should enable young people to liberate themselves- their ideas, values and options for careers.

Distance education value statement

Every institution offering distance education can evolve its value statement such as Youngstown state university, Ohio which committed to the values of:

1. Integrity and human dignity
2. Collegiality and public engagement
3. Cooperation and communication
4. Creativity and innovation
5. Community service and leadership

6. Academic and intellectual freedom
7. Pursuit of excellence
8. Electronic privacy
9. Accountability
10. Diversity

Values guiding dual mode provision

The values governing distance education provision need to be spelt out. Some institutions do this in a specific distance education policy with detailed guidelines and standards of practice.

1. A policy environment friendly to open and distance education delivery and practice must contains the following values:
2. Commitment to maintaining academic quality and standards in all programs, irrespective of modes of delivery.
3. Equal consideration for students, professional and community esteem across all modes of delivery.
4. Guaranteed access for distance education students and faculty to arrange of services comparable to those available for on campus students.
5. Sufficient training and numbers for staff to successfully deliver distance education programming
6. Commitment to providing or finding financial resources for the distance education program

Conclusion

When establishing the policy of distance education policy makers should analyse the students on-campus experience to identify areas not covered by policy but for which policy is needed, if off campus students are to experience an equivalent, if differently structured and delivered, experience to their on-campus colleagues. Institutions can conduct a student poll or survey to find out which facilities or unofficial activities on-campus students value most as part of their overall learning experience. The results can be used to determine which areas need policy to be developed for distance learners.

Policy developed to foster informal off- campus activities for distance education students can guide policy development for the same activities on campus to improve overall institutional practice.

References

1. www.ysuedu/distance learning
2. Nada Dabbagh "The online learner characteristics and pedagogical implications", contemporary issues in technology in distance education(online serial),7(3)
3. http://www.fernuni-hagenide/ICDE/D-2001
4. www.col.org/resources/publications/training resources/ knowledge/par
5. www.naac.org.nic.in

19

Factors Affecting Quality in Distance Education

Introduction

Nowadays, there is a vast and rapid growth of distance learning at all levels of education to that extend that it moves from being a marginal to becoming an integral part of the overall educational and training provisions(Moore, 2002; UNESCO, 2002). This means the significant number of learners all over the world receive their education by means of distance learning programs. But various factors are affecting the quality of distance education. Our students come from various backgrounds. Few factors affect the performance of students. The factors like number of the learner enrolled, size of the curriculum, number of year over which courses are offered without change and more year material used, the greater danger that they will became outdated. Language factor, socio-economical factor, institutional factor, income factor, non-academic factor, school factor, classroom factor, home factor and few other factors also affects the quality of distance education. This paper focused on institutional factor, language factors and socio-economic factors.

Objectives of the Study

1. To study the various factors affecting the quality in distance education
2. To study various factors affecting in graduate, post graduate and research level students
3. To study institutional factor affects the quality in distance education
4. To study the socio-economical factor affects the quality of distance education
5. To study the language factors affects the quality of distance education
6. To implement in the teaching and learning activities of the distance education

Statement of the Problem

Factors affecting quality in distance education in graduate and post graduate and research level students

Need of the Study

The attitudes of the students are changing day-by-day, and the methods of teaching technologies are also changing continuously. Numerous factors are affecting the quality in distance education. We should give importance to distance education student also. Among the number of factor the institutional and socio-economic factors also affects the quality of distance education.

Scope of the Study

The present study is intended to identify what are the institutional factors, language factor and socio-economic factors affects the quality in distance education

Various Factors Affecting Quality of Distance Education

Many factor are affecting the quality of distance education, particularly this paper focused only three factors. They are institutional factor, language factor and socio-economic factors.

Institutional Factor

1. Stop outs and dropouts of the students affect the quality of distance education. Here, stop outs are those who leave universities and return to it sometime later. Dropouts are students who leave and do not return to universities.
2. Lack of peer group of interactions
3. Limited number of seminars and workshops
4. Limited number of practical classes for the science students
5. Stagnation of the students many years affects the quality of distance education
6. Inadequate library books for the distance learning students
7. *The number of years over which courses are offered without change.* The text, audio, video or computerized formats is that the material then exists as a more or less permanent record, and can be used again and again to teach successive cohorts of students.
8. A further problem is that the more years the materials are used, the greater the danger that they will become outdated. This is likely to be more serious in some subjects (e.g. computing, social sciences, education) than in others (basic mathematics and history).
9. There is no strict in the attendance during the personal contact program
10. Involvement in research work without a sound basic knowledge in research methodology

11. Below average students getting pass marks or highest mark due to liberal valuation without enough subject knowledge.

Language Factor

Almost all the students have done their research work in English, Which is not their mother tongue. Students feel difficult to understand the subject matter and more difficult to write even single sentence properly. Thus the language factor too much has affected successful completion of the Post Graduate Degrees and research works.

Socio-economical Factor

There are various reasons why students drop out of their courses. Some reasons involve socioeconomic Factor, which are beyond the control of the university. Although Price et.al. (1992) states "The attrition rate is an indication of the quality of education that the institution offers'. This is only so if the reasons are due to factors that can be influenced by the teaching institution. Our students come from various backgrounds. The main factors affecting the provision of distance Education to the majority of the student population that drops out of the formal system are students Ability to afford our fees, home environment, community attitude to education and other social factors. The Higher Education sector needs to shift its focus from the traditional site-based learning to take distance education to the people. This means that instead of students coming to centralized learning institutions, educational services will be taken to them. Some of the factors are beyond our control.

1. We look at some of the socio-economic factors like home and study background. The majority of our students live in rural communities where the best method of contact is the postal system.

2. Students belongs to poor family and students from interior rural areas suffering due to inadequate transport facilities, lack of computer knowledge, lack of browsing centers etc.

3. Those Students houses contain a single room for all the purpose like cooking, bed room, store room, reading room etc, these kinds of factors definitely affects the education because they gets easy diversion from their studies
4. For students living in rural areas the situation is even worse. Students who live in rural areas, apart from a lack of electrification, will also lack basic learning support facilities such as libraries and peers with whom they can discuss their learning experiences.
5. Apart from their own study difficulties, most of them will also be expected to contribute to the economic welfare of the family. Finding time for private study in such cases is an enormous task for anybody.
6. Nowadays one of the reason for failure of our students include lack of place for study in the house or Neighbourhood, homes usually busy with relatives throughout the day, and sometimes drop in motivation due to lack of support from their family members.
7. People of all ages work in various degrees in producing food for their family or for sale. Sometimes education is the last thing on their minds. Community attitude to education was found to be one of the social Factors that can encourage or discourage the learning efforts of our students studying at a distance and on their own. Full time students have the advantage of peer and other support services.
8. The financial burden of coping with the tuition fees may be too much for most families. And unfortunately, there are no Government funded scholarships for distance education at the moment. There is a National Scholarship scheme established only for full time students in the universities.
9. Mature aged students may have family responsibilities which will limit the time available for study. If they are working the only time available for study is after work. But, this is also the time they may have to share with family responsibilities.

10. Individual motivation for study and reasons why students enrolled in the first place will determine how far a student will go even when support is not available.

Conclusion and Recommandation

In order to develop the quality in distance education, universities should follow some of the remedies like

a) Provide printed material on research methodologies and other subjects that should be adequate necessary Materials.

b) Conduct more seminars and workshops. Such face to face sessions will provide opportunities for peer group interactions and discussions which in turn will result in motivation and psychological boost.

c) Develop a research culture among student

d) Few universities not restricted for the registration of admission. So students are registered throughout the year, it is suggested to allocate a specific time period for the registration for graduate, Post Graduate and research students. It would also be helpful to organize seminars and workshops for the initial year, the lengthy time gap between the submission of thesis and the viva was a problem that was revealed. Such a delay may lead to student Stress. The viva should be conducted within a specific time frame after submission of the thesis.

e) As their home environment of some students is not conducive to research studies, it is necessary to create a suitable atmosphere in the university premises by providing a study area with necessary facilities.

f) A section from the Open University library could be allocated to a resource study room and is equipped.With Electronic media such as computers, internet and e – mail facilities etc. Researchers should be allocated to take their own study material into this area. The library facilities should be upgraded to have a better collection of books that are useful for research work.

g) To minimize the language barrier faced by the researchers, the language department of Open University could introduce an English course to develop academic reading and writing skills. Such short term courses were once conducted for internal staff members for few years. Such comprehensive courses could be offered to both internal and external students, who are engaged in research studies. They need such assistance to improve their language skills.

h) In the competitive world student must develop various skill like computer knowledge, internet, spoken English kind of approach to other officials etc,.

i) Universities should concentrate and increase the practical classes for the science students

j) Stagnation of the students many years, affects the quality of distance education, so open universities should take necessary steps

k) Adequate library books should be provide for the distance learning students

l) More years materials should be avoid

m) Open and distance education universities should show some strict in the attendance during the personal contact program in order to develop attitudes on studies among the students.

n) Liberal valuation must be change in to little strict due to increase the subject knowledge of the students

o) Guides should help their students for the research work and they must create involvement among the students

To implement these types of remedies in the field of distance education Instead normal method of teaching is very essential to develop the quality of distance education.

References

1. http://www.scrind.com/doc/33645148/factorsaffecting
2. http://www.irrodl.org/index
3. http://www.iitk.ac.inresearchindistancelearning
4. H:\Distance education India, universities, courses distance education India.htm
5. H:\FACTORS AFFECTING STUDENTS PERFORMANCE.htm
6. H:\factors affecting the cost of open and distance learningUNESCOeducation.ht
7. H:\institutional factors affects intention to withdraw from distance learning programs in the kingdom of Saudi Arabia the case of Arab open university

20

The Effect of Service Quality Factors on Educational Performance Through Distance Education

Introduction

Today due to the remarkable development of computers and information technology, the overall business environment has changed significantly as the digital culture via the Internet spreads in general society and the traditional industrial structure greatly changes.

This phenomenon appears prominently in the education sector and as online education business with the advantages that can escape from the constraints of time and space compared to traditional offline education environment and can save educational expenses and self-learning approach education to lead education by oneself is possible gets the limelight, government agencies and Internet companies are actively getting into telecommunications education.

As teaching method that meets the needs of such education and training, communication education training via the Internet transcending time and space such as distance education, communication education, e-Learning etc. is spreading.

If you look at Korea, as a representative means of such individual-led learning, Distance Education Training is being operated by being divided into typical Web-based communications training (Web based training) and Communication Training using mails (hereinafter referred to as 'mail communication training').

According to the Vocational Education Development Project Status by Department of Labor in 2000, in case of education and training in some developed countries, Communication education Training accounts of all education training courses and if you look in the form of education training, mail communication training occupies more than communication education using the Internet.

A lot of studies on Distance Education and service quality of e-Learning have been conducted up to now but existing researches on mail communication training, which can be said as one category of distance education but is somewhat different from Distance Education or e-Learning in the nature or characteristics are insufficient.

Therefore, the purpose of this study is to find out service quality level of mail communication training through existing prior studies on service quality of Distance Education and e-Learning and explore factors that should be considered to improve educational outcomes of learners and clarify which implications can practically be given to mail communication training.

The Concept of Mail Communication Training

Mail communication training is one of the types of distance education that learning is carried out by using postal system, guidebooks and teaching materials made by print-based materials.

Therefore, first let us look at what distance education is in order to understand mail communication training. Defined in the broad sense, distance education means teaching methods utilizing all kinds of media except for face-to-face education.

Also, distance education in the narrow sense is the education system of new concept providing demander-oriented educational service through learning activities taking place in cyberspace of time and place users want by using a variety of multimedia information technology based on the Internet and are the concept created in the course of information and communication technology breakthrough (Jeong, Gi-hong, 2002).

Like this, definition about distance education can be largely divided into four kinds depending on the highlighted aspects.

First, a position to highlight media thinks that training activities are carried out using media as a means of filling the gap, assuming that the core of distance education is the physical distance between people providing educational services and people receiving education services

Second, a position to highlight course characteristics by which distance education is operated defines distance education as a form of systematically supporting autonomous learning of learners.

This shows that learning types of learners away from education service providers are basically autonomous and emphasizes activities supporting self-study.

Third, this is an aspect that stresses interactive characteristics of distance education. It says that because most communication of distance education is carried out without direct meeting between education service providers and learners, interactive communication between education service providers and learners is essential to facilitate the progress of the learning process. While the information and communications technologies are highlighted as intermediaries facilitating this, 'instructive two-way interaction' (Holmberg, 1994) is valued in distance education by printing materials as well.

Fourth, this is a position to define distance education through comparison with other existing education forms. Unlike face-to-face education, distance education keeps the characteristics that has physical distance between education service providers and learners, gets organizational support in the operating process unlike self-study or informal private learning and pursues two-way interaction through the means of media. (Oh, Young-hoon and Son, Yu-mi, 2001).

Judging from the definition on distance education we've seen so far, mail communication training is common with distance education from a point of view that education service providers and learners are physically apart and organizational support is fulfilled but is a different education form from a point of view that it uses the media, mail communication as intermediary means to fill the gap.

Service Quality of Mail Communication Training

Looking at studies on web-based educational services, Bae, Mi-kyung's study using SERVPERF measures indicated that service quality measures consist of 6 levels such as tangibility, reliability, responsiveness, confirmation, sympathy and ease of use (Bae, Mi-kyung, 2002) and Jo, Jong-won's study using slightly modified questionnaire indicated that they consist of 6 levels such as tangibility, reliability, responsiveness, confirmation, sympathy and interactivity (Jo, Jong-won, 2004). Unlike these studies, Song, Jong-tae's study measuring service quality of distance education by adding online education service assessment items based on R-SERVQUAL presented 6 service quality levels such as exterior facilities, interactivity, problem solving, convenience, providing information and safeness (Song, Jong-tae, 2003) and Kim, Yoon-kyoung's study assessing service quality of e-Learning by reorganizing questionnaire based on studies of Yoo, Pyeong-joon and Bae, Mi-kyung presented 6 levels of service quality such as tangibility, reliability, responsiveness, confirmation, convenience (Kim, Yoon-kyoung, 2003).

In addition to these, service quality levels of distance education and e-Learning sectors are being presented through recent many studies.

Like this, looking at studies on service quality of web-based education service (distance education and e-Learning), we can see that each researcher presents different levels. Also, mail communication training conducts information provision and learning assessment etc. by using Internet sites but it is a little bit different from distance education and e-Learning from a point of view that learning process is based on printing materials.

Conclusion

It categorizes evaluation of education programs of Kirkpatrick into 4 steps such as learner responses, achievement, field application and final result. Learner reponses of the first step are satisfaction on instructors, learning contents, textbooks, learning environment etc.

The second step is the one that measures achievement of learning goals and the third step is measurement about practicing what they learned in the field and the last final result is that what results would be brought when what they learned was applied in the field (Oh, In-kyeong, 2000).

Studies of Jeong, In-seong and Choi, Seong-hui (1999) presented satisfaction and degree of education effect awareness as result factors affecting education effectiveness of web-based virtual training.

Also, Jeong, Yong-geun's study measured meeting and inspiration of growth needs and improvement of ability to perform duties as factors affecting corporate training result.

Reference

1. Kim, Yoon-kyoung, (2003) "Study on e-Learning Service Quality and e-Loyalty", SookMyung Women's University, *Master's Thesis.*

2. Bae, Mi-kyung, (2002) "Study on e-Learning Service Quality: Centering on Learning Portal site service", Korea University, *Master's Thesis.*

3. Song, Jong-tae, (2003) "An Influence that Service Quality has on Customer Satisfaction, Repurchase Intention and Oral Communication", Wonkwang University, *Master's Thesis.*

4. Oh, In-kyoung, (2000) "Evaluation on Educational_ Effectiveness_of_Web-Based Education within Companies According to Four Steps Assessment Model of Kirkpatrick", *Corporate Education Research*, 2, (1), Pp.71-92.

5. Oh, Young-Hoon, Son, Yoo-Mi, (2001) "*Problems and Development Plan of Communication Training Using Mail Media*" Korea Research Institute for Vocational Education and Training.

6. Lee, Young-Joon, (2002) understanding of factor analysis, *Seokjeong*, Pp. 86-89.

7. Im, Jong-won, Park, Hyoung-jin, Gang, Myung-soo, (2003) Marketing Research Methodology, *Bobmunsa*, pp 31-35.

8. Jo, Jong-won, (2004) "A Study on Influence that Service Quality Attributes have on Educational Effectiveness in Corporate e-Learning", Hankuk University of Foreign Studies, *Master's Thesis.*

9. Jeong, Gi-hong, (2002) "A Study on Development Direction of Cyber University and Distance Education", Kyonggi University Graduate School of Information and Communication, *Master's Thesis.*

10. Jeong, In-seong, (1999) "Open Distance Education and Information and Communication Engineering", *Kyoyookbook.*

11. Jeong, In-seong, Choi, Seong-hui, (1999) "Effect factor Analysis of Online Open Education", *The Journal of Education Research.*37,(1), Pp.369-388.

12. Jeong, Yong-geun, (1998) "A Study on Determining Factors of Corporate Education Training Performance", Sogang University Graduate School of Business, *Master's Thesis.*

13. J. Joseph Cronin and Steven A. Tayor, (1992) "Measuring Service Quality: A reexamination and Extension", *Journal of Marketing*, 56, Pp 55-68.

21

Strategies to Enhance Interactivity in Distance Education

Introduction

The distance education format challenges teachers to develop a learning environment that places more responsibility on the student to accomplish academic tasks with minimal teacher assistance. This early form of distance education moved the learning frontiers to the learners' home. Successful distance education system involves interactivity between teachers and students, between students and the environment, and among students themselves, as well as active learning in the classroom. Garrison (1990) argued that the quality and integrity of the educational process depends upon sustained, two-way communication. Although such commitments are time consuming in terms of design, preparation, and teaching, they are necessary for student success in distance education.

Distance Education

Distance education represents a unique context for the teaching and learning process. Spitzer (1998) notes that "those involved in distance education grossly underestimate the difficulty involved in changing deeply entrenched teaching and learning habits, and consequently we grossly underestimate the difficulty of changing from a traditional classroom environment to a distance learning context" It represents the connectivity the students feel with the distance teachers, aides, counsellors, facilitators and their peers. In some forms of distance education, this is practically nonexistent, but most cases, it is considered important. Historically, the learning process has taken place with the infrastructure of institutions such as schools, university campuses, technical colleges, etc. The need to be part of such institutions was driven by the notion that to access information and knowledge, a learner had to be present where the teacher was. The first separation between the teacher and the student occurred with correspondence education, which offered information and knowledge mediated by some form of media, usually print.

Distance Educator Competencies

Salmon (2000) offers superb insights into essential teacher competencies from her action research studies on Computer Mediated Conferencing (CMC). Salmon utilizes research studies to develop a comprehensive chart of five e-moderator competencies:

Understanding of online process-understand how to promote group work, pace online discussions, experiment with new ideas

Technical skills-use software to facilitate student interaction by monitoring student messages and create conferencing opportunities

Online communication skills- able to effectively interact with students by using concise and clear messages that encourage academic dialog and personalise the online experience

Content expertise- credible subject matter knowledge and experience to share comments/questions that stimulate lively debate

Personal characteristics-able to adapt to different teaching situations and demonstrates a genuine excitement about online learning.

Importance of Interaction in Distance Education

As educators refine their philosophy of distance learning, they are concerned about sustaining interactivity in their educational process. Today's distance learning theories are built upon the premise that teachers will assist their students to become self-directed and independent (Moore, 1990). Learners must assume responsibility for their educational experiences, but independent study has natural limitations. If learners do not receive adequate teacher feedback and reinforcement, students will not always know whether they possess an accurate knowledge of their subject matter. A primary goal of distance education is to promote self-directed attitudes while discouraging excessive dependency upon the instructor (Milheim, 1993). Computer-mediated education creates unique risks for both tutors and learners. Tutors can face heavy workloads from large online classes that require large amounts of personal emails, phone calls, and discussion forum comments. Learners devalue their personal knowledge and life experiences, their online contributions can become more driven by an obligation to get through the experience .Collis (1998) shared the following four vital instructional principles for distance education:

1. Both learner and educator play an active and unique role in the educational process.
2. The process of creatively acquiring knowledge involves human interaction and learner competence.
3. Contemporary models of learning support learned centered instruction that encourages self-assessment, personal reflection, and elicit learner articulation of their ideas.
4. The learning environment should maximize meaningful and reflective interactions while providing.

Enhancing Interactivity in Distance Education

1. Promote critical thinking

Students use written comments to share conceptual knowledge with their classmates and teachers. The reading and writing process does promote cognitive and meta-cognitive skills due to the opportunity to reflect before responding to comments (Hannafin, Hill and Land, 1997). Online dialog over written messages can offer more in-depth intellectual inquiry than face-to-face conversations which usually encourage immediate responses. Instructors must strive to develop questions that are interesting and reflect a diversity of ideas to stimulate online dialogs. Online educators are faced with various barriers to quality dialogs such as having a discussion that is not focused or ones which are intellectually shallow. Instructors must use conversational techniques to sharpen dialog focus by providing direction, offering commentary that sorts ideas according to their relevance. The dialogue can be enriched by instructors who offer a diverse range of questions that cause individuals to examine their assumptions, beliefs, ideas and rationale. Instructors should post comments that indicate that they honour a multiple of perspectives.

2. Relevant and engaging lectures

Traditional instructors are sometimes placed into difficult circumstances when they are required to teach an online class with little or no formal training. Often, they must post their lecture notes for their students to read while striving to facilitate a discussion based on the lecture notes. Also, it places pressure on the teacher to produce an excellent lecture because students will have plenty of time to examine the lecture and discuss its contents. Lectures can be used to personalize the learning environment when instructors develop a conversational style that reflects their personality. Additionally, it is wise to include diverse discussion questions with lectures that explore vital content issues and enable students to refer to their work and life experiences. Shearer, (2003) stresses "without the proper use of sequence, pace, and feedback, the learner perceives little control over the learning environment, and without other means of timely interaction with the instructor (e.g. by phone or fax) the psychological distance may feel immense". Instructors learn to translate their knowledge and wisdom into a lecture that effectively communicates. It takes time to create quality lectures which reflect creativity and capture the imagination and attention of students.

3. Positive affirmation of student work

Instructors can promote greater online participation by affirming their students' abilities and knowledge. The teacher can make positive comments about an individuals' expertise in a public forum such as a newsgroup and through private email messages. The key is to be sincere and share positive comments with every student in the class. Distance learners appreciate being recognized for their accomplishments and online classes offer numerous opportunities for instructors to affirm quality work.

4. Integrate stories into the class discussions

Online students want classes that stress the human side of learning. The author has found that students really enjoy stories from the teacher's life because it makes the class more personal and assists them with their academic work. In a doctoral research class, it would be a good opportunity for the instructor to share stories that provides insights on how he or she arrived at their dissertation topic. The wise instructor will use short stories to generate lively discussion within the class on a variety of social issues.

5. Provide students with flexibility

Instructors must be careful not to provide excessive structure to their classes that eliminates the potential for students making critical decisions about their assignments. The term flexibility refers to making the learning more relevant to the student's needs or circumstances. The instructional emphasis is to make the learning experiences more individualized. Collis (1998) relates, “These relate to time flexibility, content flexibility, entry and completion flexibility, instructional-approach flexibility, learning-resource flexibility, technology-use flexibility, interactivity and communication flexibility, course-logistics flexibility, as well as location flexibility.”

Conclusion

Today’s professional development programs for online teachers would benefit from interactivity research studies and tailor their curriculum to better prepare their instructors. Teachers need the expertise to develop a class structure that stimulates social interaction and affirms rigorous academic standards while fostering independent learning skills. Successful distance education system involves interactivity between teachers and students, between students and the environment, and among students themselves, as well as active learning in the classroom

Reference

1. AGGRAWAL.J.C. (1996), Teachers and education in a developing society, Vikas publishing house pvt , New Delhi.
2. SHASHIPRABHASAHARMA. (2003), Teacher Education principles, Theories and practices, Kanishka Publishers, New Delhi.
3. www.coe.int/compass
4. http://www.ln.edu.hk/tlc/level2/td.htm.
5. www.un-gaid.org/tabid/883

22

Quality Enhancement in Distance Education For Life Long Learning

Introduction

Education doesn't have any retirement. It is a lifelong process. As it is a lifelong process, can all the learners join in regular courses to learn new things? It is not possible for anybody to pursue education in regular stream though all consider that education is a lifelong process. The only answer that we have to prove that education is a lifelong process is through distance education. The learners of distance education are almost heterogeneous. Most of them have seen the life in different perspectives. Their expectations through distant education may be manifold. Very ordinary items for learning will not live up to the expectations of the distant learners. There are two types of students available in a classroom. One is 'head hanging' and the other one is 'leg shaking'. Those who don't understand what is taught will hang their heads in disappointment and for whom the teaching doesn't include any new information will shake their legs. That way, if better learning opportunities are not there in the distance education material then that will lead the learners to a dishevelled approach on the course and on the distance education pattern. So, it is mandatory on the part of the universities that offer courses through distant mode should consider that their qualitative input alone can make the learners to have faith in lifelong learning.

Distance Education

Distance education is the most welcome-guest for the drop-outs and for the working people. The concept of low performers join in distance education does not exist. Indian families with a large numbers in their folds are forced to compromise with giving their children the required education, so as to put them to stay independent. Distance education is the only resort where the dream of aspiring to get degrees can be achieved. It is more flexible as the compulsory programmes are scheduled in a convenient time for both the teachers and the learners without disturbing their regular activities. It not only helps the learners to get better job prospects but also enriches the individuals. As the continuing programmes are carried out in convenient time more importance is given to content and the goals. Distance education can take help from the technological advancement in making its learners not inferior to learners of regular stream.

Distance Education and Its Academic Credit

In the United States of America it is mandatory for many industry boards, accreditation agencies and associations to have Continuing Professional Education (CPE) for licensure or certification. It is strongly felt there that people should not stop learning even after securing a better job. In India, if we compare the quality difference between the entry behaviour and terminal behaviour of our teachers, we are startled to note that either both are at the same level or the terminal behaviour is far inferior to the entry behaviour. It is because, most people may think that getting job is their priority and enhancing knowledge is not stipulated on them. The ministry of Human Resource Development is taking many steps to improve quality in higher education. Teachers in colleges and universities have to show some improvement by way of acquiring some degrees, presenting papers in national and international conferences of this kind and much more. For these teachers distance education also can become a handy for scoring the required credits.

Life Long Learning

In recent times the concept of lifelong learning is getting popularity. Organizations at present are challenged to quickly adapt the requirement of its employees in learning forever. Through the lifelong learning process, individuals develop the capacity for tackling the problems that they encounter. The most important features of lifelong learning are duration, learner-centred perspective, multi-level and multi-subject learning, and open access. The crest of lifelong learning is that the individuals learn from cradle to grave and that the individual progress from one level of learning to the next level of learning throughout his life time. Lifelong learning focuses on the learners rather than giving importance to the teachers. It is not that the learners are not required for lifelong learning, but he facilitates the learning. He guides the learners on the ways to acquire different learning items. Lifelong learners need more options to choose and the time that suits their convenient. Lifelong learning activities are also aimed at multiple learning styles. Lifelong learning includes skill training, credential requirements as well as social interests. Lifelong learning has to be available to all individuals regardless of age, race, ability, basic qualifications, and so on. Universities must take steps to ensure that learning activities are accessible to anyone who is interested in participating.

Global Need

Education is no more restricted to any particular country. It has become a global phenomenon. Distance education materials have to be in a global standard. Our graduates get job in other countries and the graduates of other countries get job in our country testifies that the learning need and the teaching strategies are same all over the world. The materials for the distant learners should be aimed at preparing the learners to an open situation. To put precisely, they have to be globally prepared. There was an article in the Hindu, very recently, that students from Tamil Nadu are not coming out successful in IIT entrance examinations. It was reasoned out that our questions in the +2 examinations are not aimed at testing the calculation part of scientific application. It was further reported that when in one year the questions came for calculation, it was vehemently opposed, it seems. From this episode it is inferred that our +2 students are not globally prepared.

Quality Enhancement in Distance Education

It is necessary that the concept of distance education should reach even the people of underprivileged. The quality of distance education can be enhanced by offering more branches of studies and bring in the usefulness of science and technology into it. The content of the learning items in distance education should have relevance in today's juncture. A set of well trained teachers have to be involved in imparting these learning items to the learners very effectively. Activities like making aware of available jobs for the pursued course by conducting campus interviews will definitely give opportunities to the learners to know about the prosperity of the course pursued and also it can give satisfying confidence to the learners. The package in the distance education should also include the scope for getting their problems redressed. Apt personalities of repute can be involved in distance programmes, so as to give chances for the learners to receive first-hand information from the persons practising them. This will encourage the distant learners to the maximum. Programmes like interior decoration, craft and other livelihood activities that can empower womanhood should also be included in the distance education. Many women in India are still deprived of pursuing distance education in response to social compulsion and for them useful on-line programmes have to be formulated.

Conclusion

Quality enhancement in distance education is the need of the hour. India can aspire for increasing the percentage of people pursue higher education is mainly through distance education. India, being one of the most populous countries can depend on educating its subjects prominently by distance education. If at all India is in the counting of becoming a developed country, it is possible only through making its people to have faith in lifelong learning. The concept of lifelong learning can be sustained only when the distance programmes of qualitative in nature. So, the institutions that offer distance education programmes should necessarily maintain quality to make the lifelong learning possible.

23

Enhancing Quality in Open and Distance Learning

Introduction

In the present competitive and knowledge intensive society ensuring lifelong learning opportunities for all is becoming very essential. It is becoming a necessity for every individual to continually update his skills in order to meet the rising demands of the global world and to adapt themselves to the changing lifestyle. Education today must be able to produce globally competent citizens and this is not possible with educating them only for a specified period of time. To make everyone meet the challenges of the globally changing world it is essential that they learn more than mere subjects. But all this cannot be dealt with the formal sector of education alone. Educating everyone irrespective of age, caste, gender, social, financial and physical constraints is something beyond the capacity of the formal sector of education alone. Thus in order to cater to the rising demands posed on education by globalization, one of the best alternatives is the Open and Distance Learning (ODL). ODL is now gaining world-wide acceptance and significance because of its diverse potentiality and flexibility. But with the increasing demand for ODL it should be made sure that the quality of education being imparted through distance learning is superior and that it is not made a mere commodity. Thus, while meeting with the quantitative needs of our society, the quality should not be compromised with, because there is absolutely no substitute to quality of education.

Quality in Education

Quality is a very complex term and has many dimensions to it. In the ODL system, according to Gandhi (2009), quality means attainment of the expected levels of knowledge and skills which are tools for further learning by actual work experience necessary for managing the learner's personal and social transaction in day–to-day life. This quality is to be attained by all distance learners, in a given time frame. Today more and more students prefer ODL to the formal educational sector of education for higher learning. But as per IGNOU (2009), the problems of efficiency, equity, quality and benchmarking of the ODL system still persist. All this is reflected in the low acceptability of students from the ODL system in reputed traditional Universities for higher degrees. Further, the students of the ODL system find gainful employment with difficulty. So it's high time that these loopholes are plugged and quality requirements be taken care of seriously.

The following are a few recommendations on how quality in ODL can be improved and strengthened:

Infrastructure: For any kind of an educational system to sustain and flourish a proper infrastructure is what is needed. Infrastructural facilities should be sound and strong enough to meet the rising demands of the learners. Proper space, buildings, furniture, equipments and all other material requirements needed as per syllabus and courses should be there. Institutes and study centres should be setup in places which are easily accessible to all In ODL what is most important is the technological infrastructure. According to Enuku&Ojogwu (2006) and Rennie& Mason (2007), in developing countries, the growth of ODL has been severely deterred due to the lack of technological infrastructure. Thus computers with latest software and internet connection should be made available to all learners in the institute where classes are conducted. Video-conferencing and the use of radio, television and web/satellite based communication technologies should be promoted at all Open University centres especially at the remote and rural areas. But while providing all this, what has to be frequently done is the continuous up gradation of the technology as per the changes taking place in the globalised world. Technological infrastructure which is outdated is of no use. Thus a committee should be set up to deal with such issues. It should monitor and assess all centres on the above criteria and make sure that distance education centres are equipped with the latest technological infrastructure.

Curriculum: This is one of the major determinants of quality. A strong learner centered and flexible curriculum as per the changing demands of the globalised world is the need of the hour. But Dev (2010) feels that some of the ODL course curricula are irrelevant to the real life needs of the underprivileged population. A large number of education seekers are denied access because of the irrelevance of the programs. Thus courses in ODL should be so designed that it actually benefits those for whom it is intended to-the marginalized, disadvantaged, drop-outs, differently-baled and so on. Instead of mere certificate courses more vocational/technical courses which would develop practical work skills should be promoted. It should offer courses which would help every individual undertaking the same to compete and survive in the globalised world thus creating opportunities for self-employment and entrepreneurship. State open universities should also keep in mind the topographical peculiarities and resource availability while planning the curricula. Courses should be of regional relevance. There should also be wide range of choice in subjects from which learners can choose as per their needs and demands. Only then would the learners be able to make maximum use of their education and genuinely improve their own lives as well as contribute to the growth of the nation too. And it is when this happens can we say that the quality of education imparted was good.

Instructional strategy: For effective curriculum transaction what is of utmost importance is none other than effective instructional strategies. In ODL it is through electronic/print media that learning takes place mostly. Multimedia approach is widely being used. But it must be made sure that whatever be the approach, learner centred activities should be promoted. Moiduser et al. (2000) found that many online programs do not exhibit evidence of innovative pedagogical approaches, such as using constructivist learning principles like those of cooperative and collaborative learning. Thus group discussions, cooperative learning techniques, collaborative learning techniques, seminars and project works should be the main strategies of teaching. Such techniques arouse a genuine interest in the learner to learn and also help him to apply what he has learnt to real life situations thereby promoting the quality of education being imparted. A panel of experts for the same should be set up. Every state can have a separate panel and apart from designing strategies they should also evaluate how effective the strategies are. Timely monitoring and evaluation, frequent interactions with students and tracking students performance in exams would definitely help to find out whether these strategies are actually being used in ODL centres and if so how effectively.

Faculty: Teachers in ODL have to be selected as per the norms used by regular institutes. There should be no compromise on quality of teachers being posted. Apart from recruitments it also has to be seen that the in-service teachers are getting fully fledged opportunities for their professional growth. They should have opportunities for attending workshops, seminars and conferences on a timely basis. Training should be given to the faculty so as to help them develop the desired practical and technological skills needed. They should be regularly updated on the changing technologies and thus adequate resources and technological infrastructure have to be provided to the faculty for the same.

Delivery of learning materials: This is also equally important. Here most of the learning is through multimedia and it has to be made sure that the delivery method is appropriate for the students and the curriculum. Students should have easy access to latest technologies so that they can get the desired learning materials from the media. Learners should be taught the basic skills needed for being able to use multimedia for learning on their own. The instructional strategies and learning materials should be designed accordingly so as to suit the technology used to deliver the course. The print materials have to be dispatched on time and made sure that all students get it. Open universities should set up a particular working group for the same. They have to accountable for delivery of print materials to all on time. Another group can be set up for dealing with delivery of materials via multimedia. Regular monitoring of these groups and feedback from students will help in keeping up the quality in delivery of learning materials.

Assessment and Evaluation: It is only through proper assessment that one can understand how effective is the education imparted to the learner. But the assessment should be such that it assesses the learner throughout the course of study. Assignments and projects can be evaluated online. Seminars and other group presentations can be evaluated when contact classes are conducted. Online examinations should be conducted on a regular basis. But assessment should not be limited to academics alone. Along with that, the overall development of the leaner should also be assessed. The different type of skills developed-general and those specific to field of study-also have to be assessed. For this it would be better if every open learning institute specifies the expected knowledge and skills a student is expected to develop after completion of their courses. So then after completion of course it can be assessed whether the desired skills have been developed or not. But all these have to be maintained in records.

Student support system: Students must be given the desired technical support and apart from that they should be provided facilities for attending contact classes and meeting subject experts whenever needed. All the information and data needed should be available online so that students can access it from any place and any time without difficulty. Also enquiry centres should be setup at all regional centres where students can easily approach personally or through mail and thus clear their doubts and queries regarding courses, syllabi, registration, payment of fees, examination schedules, declaration of results etc. Grievance cells, where students can address their problems and difficulties faced in the ODL system, should be made functional more efficiently and effectively.

Employment: The employment opportunity of its learners of is a very important element that helps determine the quality of distance education imparted. To what extent these learners are able to get placed along with regular candidates is very crucial. Thus the institutes should maintain records regarding the placement of their students. Apart from that the number of learners who have been able to get self-employed successfully should also be mentioned. All these would give a clearer picture of how successful the ODL courses have been and what all changes need to be implemented so as to increase the competency and employment opportunities of their learners. Also the State Open Universities can start some collaboration with regional factories/industries in order to promote campus selection.

The Distance Education Council set up under the Indira Gandhi National Open University Act has been assigned the regulatory role for the open & distance learning universities and the higher educational ODL institutions. The DEC examines the working of these universities and institutions in all its aspects before granting recognition. It is likely that the DEC also undertakes assessment and accreditation of the open & distance learning institutions in India in the near future (Gandhe, 2009). Along with that the DEC can also setup **quality assurance cells** in every state and work together for assessing and enhancing quality of ODL institutes in every state. This will help in strengthening quality of ODL institutes.

Research: Research in ODL should be promoted. More studies should be taken up on the ODL institutes and universities, its functioning, efficiency, present status, quality assurance methods, curricula relevance, instructional strategies used and so on. Only if in-depth studies are done on these areas can the lacunae in every area be found out and dealt with successfully ultimately leading to the enhancement in the quality of these institutes and universities.

A well-defined budget and financial plan: Finally this is what is very essential if the above mentioned recommendations have to be put into practice. Without proper funding quality enhancement measures cannot be implemented successfully. So the central and state governments should make sure that an appropriate amount be kept apart for ODL alone.

Conclusion

Education imparted should help every individual make his life comfortable and environment richer. It should help everyone contribute to the development of the country and when this happens we can say that the quality of education imparted is good. The quality of education being imparted, whether formal or informal, is a major issue of concern in the present day and it has to be accounted for and looked into seriously. Few suggestions have been mentioned above which would help in enhancing quality in ODL. But quality can actually be achieved only when these suggestions are put into practice. Effective implementation is what is needed than mere lectures. But for that it requires the concerted effort of everyone-learners, teachers, educationists, academicians, researchers, policy-makers, politicians, industrialists and the common man. So it's high time that we all come forward and work together for putting into practice what has always been only talked of till today, thus making the dream of quality education come true.

References

1. Dev, K. (2010), "Social Justice: Disabilities: Knowledge and Skill Acquisition From a Distance: Meeting the Changing Demands of Disadvantaged", Paper presented at the Sixth Pan

Commonwealth Forum on Open Learning (PCF6), Kochi, Kerala ason 02/01/11 retrieved from www.pcf6.net/pages/fp/zIN1214.doc

2. Enuku, E. U., &Ojogwu, C. N. (2006), "Information and communication technology (ICT) in the service of the national open university in Nigeria", *Education, 127*(2), 187-195
3. Dirani, K.M. & Yoon, S.W. (2009), "Exploring Open Distance Learning in a Jordanian University: A Case Study", *The International Review of Research in Open and Distance Learning, Vol.10, No.2* as on 27/01/2011
4. Gandhe, S.K. (2009), "Quality Assurance in Open and Distance Learning in India" as on 21/01/11 retrieved from http://www.openpraxis.com/files/Gandhe%20et%20al.pdf
5. IGNOU (2009), "A Report onSelected Innovative Practices in Open and Distance Learning", New Delhi:National Centre for Innovations in Distance Education as on 28/01/11 retrieved from http://www.ignou.ac.in/ncide/Report250209.pdf
6. Moiduser et al. (2000) In Dirani, K.M. & Yoon, S.W. (2009), "Exploring Open Distance Learning in a Jordanian University: A Case Study", *The International Review of Research in Open and Distance Learning, Vol.10, No.2* as on 27/01/2011
7. Rennie, F. & Mason, R. (2007), "The development of distributed learning techniques in Bhutan and Nepal", *International Review of Research inOpen and Distance Learning, 8(1),* 1-10

24

Quality Enhancement in Distance Education For Lifelong Learning

Introduction

There two Systems ofDistance Education (i) Regular Distance Learning (II) Open Distance Learning. The Contribution of ODL in higher Education is around 25% in India. The following groups in the society are being benefited through this open Distance Learning.

School dropouts, house-wives, employed people who want to learn while earning some livelihood, people from moral areas and all those who were denied access and opportunity for formal Education due to geographical distances, Socio-economic and cultural barriers.

ODL helps to develop the huge manpower required through effective learning and planning for the betterment of the Society.

ODL is applied for Learning and development in the following ways.

1. Socio-Economic and cultural characteristics
2. Literacy educational level

3. Infrastructure facilities and trained Manpower required
4. To improve the standards on Literacy rate and educational levels
5. Action Research approach helps in the following ways.
    a) In built feedback Mechanism
    b) Quality of content
    c) Presentation and comprehension
    d) Attainment Levels
    e) Learning Styles
    f) Expectations and outcome of the Target learning etc.,

Open Dstance Learning Enchances Social Values

Education is a continual process and it can be achieved successfully with the help of distance mode of learning. Let us create a new brave world with the help of distance Education. So the distance Education should act as a powerful Institution of Social and Economic change in country. It must be continuing with full vigour in order to improve the Social status of the society. Skilful students who are unable to make use of their regular college studies can utilize these opportunities to uplift their Socio-Economic Status.

Theoretical concepts of distance education and the radical developments in information and communication technologies have accelerated the transformation of Correspondence Education in open Distance learning elevating the status and characteristics in transporting the quality education knowledge and information to the people's homes and work places and transcending the geographical distances.

Open Distance Learning is Pursuing to Createsocial Equality

1. To increase the literacy rates and educational Standards of Scholars.

2. To enhance the social economic and cultural characteristics of individual learning.
3. Availability and accessibility to electronic media by the target learners.
4. To help in assessing the projects achievement at different stages in an "Action Research" approach.
5. To Create inbuilt feed-back mechanism on all aspects like quality of content, course delivery and support services keeping in view the accessibility to e- media.
6. ODL is aiming to develop the 'huge man power' required through effective planning and utilization of the available resources.

Role of IGNOU

IGNOU is the world's largest Distance Educational Institution. It has 13 open Universities and 100 State and private run Universities cater to the Educational needs of 22% of the collegiate and higher Education populace in the country through Distance Education and the Open university mode.

This university attracts the special category of students such as prison inmates and sex workers over the recent years. The University is trying to offer on a variety of degree and certificate programmes that are not available in the regular mode of Education .

The real challenge is to integrate technology by developing required infrastructures so that the students deprived of quality Education get the benefit of knowledge Revolution. Effort is also required to create awareness among learners that distance education in no way is inferior to the conventional mode of Education.

Image building through quality programmes and better learner support services is the need of the hour. This needs to be done through publicity and promotional activities, development of publicity materials, participations in local book fairs, exhibitions etc., conducting road shows in the towns and the hinterland, usage of various media for publicity and promotional purposes such as advertisements, interviews, Panel discussions on radio , Television, Newspaper, World wide web, conduct meetings with, Policy Makers, including State Government officials, employers, parents and fellow peers working at other educational Institutions etc.,

ODL Institutions should create students alumni and arrange meetings of their students. ODL should felicitate successful students and should arrange induction programmes for new entrants and develop mechanisms for obtaining feedback from their learners, covering all aspects including courseware learners support services, evaluation methodology, relevance of the curriculum etc., Information obtained should be ploughed back for betterment and improvement in the system. ODL should create a feeling of belongingness to the Institution and contribute to the self-esteem of distance learners.

The last four decades in the history of Education can be called as the period of development of open Distance learning system. ODL Strategy can be applied effectively to any community groups like farmers, rural poor, women and artisans etc., for improving their livelihoods and standard of living , building awareness and skills development for income generation.

ODL supports not only learning resources but also removes the sense of isolation among the distance learners and promote socialization.

ODL creates a two-way communication strategies to promote interaction with teachers through assignments and other e- media accessible to the learners.

ODL elevates the status and characteristics in transporting the quality Education, knowledge and information to the people's homes and work places and transcending the geographical distances . It facilitates independent learning and thus promoting autonomy of Learning.

Conclusion

Government may take concrete steps for capacity building in ODL system, in order to increase the qualified and trained man power in the field of Distance Education and to improve the quality of Education imparted by this system. Government may take appropriate policy decisions to avoid ambiguity and anxiety among the students of Distance Education in the field of employment opportunities.

25

Technology Enabled Learning in Distance Education

Online education, a form of distance education based on Internet technologies, has emerged as a major global trend. The online environment's ability to network minds, foster reflective thinking, and create the conditions for individuals and groups working at a distance to develop communities of practice is undoubtedly its unique strength. Interaction is essential for participation in communities that generate knowledge and is rapidly becoming a quotidian expectation for learners in online learning communities. The challenge then is to develop new learning designs that sustain collaborative learning and help learners develop collaborative learning strategies applicable across evolving content domains and disciplines. The advancement of Information and Communication Technology (ICT) has a significant and profound impact on distance education. In terms of teaching and learning in distance education, where the learner and teacher are separated in time and space, ICT in the form of a web-based learning environment can support an array of instructional delivery media, utilising the effective pedagogical approaches that involve and seek the active participation of students in the construction of knowledge. Features of the World Wide Web, such as hypertexts, graphics, sound and video illustrations and the easy-to-handle point and click graphical interfaces provide an extensive environment for instructional designers to develop diverse types of learning materials. Navarro and Shoemaker (2000) studied student performance and the perception of distance learners in cyberspace in terms of their attitude towards the essential instructional technologies, their perception towards the learner–instructor and learner–learner interactions, their satisfaction and related technical problems. They discovered that students preferred the cyberspace mode of learning, as the instructional technology could stimulate the classroom experience, support collaborative learning and interactive feedback. The support made available for student– student interaction via the electronic bulletin board enabled stimulating thoughts and debates to take place and led to satisfying and effective learning experiences. The most useful function of the web from educational view is that it can be used effectively as communication medium for student collaboration an information resource, a search tool and as a medium for publication.

Online education, a form of distance education based on Internet technologies, has emerged as a major global trend. The online environment's ability to network minds, foster reflective thinking, and create the conditions for individuals and groups working at a distance to develop communities of practice is undoubtedly its unique strength. Designers must move beyond the strategies employed by "early adopters" and create educational contexts that support interaction and collaboration through technology oriented communication. Interaction is essential for participation in Distance Education that generates knowledge and is rapidly becoming a quotidian expectation for learners in online learning communities. The challenge then is to develop new learning designs that sustain collaborative learning and help learners develop collaborative learning strategies applicable across evolving content domains and disciplines.

Fundamentally, there are two distinct factors propelling the changes in ICT's and education: ICTs are radically changing the nature of work and the workplace, and more generally, the "information and knowledge revolution", combined with globalization, have created conditions in which countries that have focused on knowledge-based. The world is fast becoming a global village owing to the developments in the information and communication technology (ICT). The key instrument in this globalization, increasingly, has become the necessity of everyday life. Most of the developed countries have exploited the potentials of ICT to transform their educational landscape at the tertiary, secondary and even primary levels of school education, particularly, the instructional process (Kosakowski 1998). Generally ICT holds the opportunity to revolutionise pedagogical methods, expand access to quality education, and improve the management of education systems (World Bank 2002). .

Integration of Information Technology in Education

Industries have been able to reap significant rewards. Knowledge-based industries require an educated labour force of computer-literate individuals who themselves understand and can harness the power of ICT. In response to the demands for producing such a labour force, many countries have changed the objectives of their education system and have directed much of their attention to the development of ICT skills in schools.

(2) More specifically, ICTs offer tremendous possibilities in:

A. improving student's learning by enhancing the teaching/ learning process;
B. developing teachers' professional capability; and
C. strengthening institutional capacity.

The introduction of ICT in the education system requires careful planning. ICT, like any powerful tool, can do as much harm as good. Bad pedagogy implemented on a computer may have its harmful effects multiplied many fold by the power of the technology. Educational leaders and planners thus bear the tremendous responsibility of ensuring that the introduction of ICT is managed with great care so that the potential benefits are realised, while the dangers are eliminated or minimised.

Web Based Learning

The advancement of Information and Communication Technology (ICT) has a significant and profound impact on distance education. In terms of teaching and learning in distance education, where the learner and teacher are separated in time and space, ICT in the form of a web-based learning environment can supportan array of instructional delivery media, utilising the effective pedagogical approaches that involve and seek the active participation of students in the construction of knowledge. Features of the World Wide Web, such as hypertexts, graphics, sound and video illustrations and the easy-to-handle point and click graphical interfaces provide an extensive environment for instructional designers to develop diverse types of learning materials.

The web can also support various forms of communicative features that can connect lecturers and students for teaching and learning activities. Features such as the synchronous learning activities (computer conferencing, chats, web tutorials) and the asynchronous learning activities (e-mail, list servers and web courses) provide means of effective communication and reinforce the teaching and learning conducted through distance education. In terms of the learners' support system in distance education, the ICT in the form of a web environment is capable of supporting various interactive features that facilitate the fulfilment of the needs and requirements of the learners at a distance. The on-line course registration, on-line fee payments, general enquiries, counselling services, virtual notice boards and the chat facility are known to be contributory to efficient student management and administration, resulting in the provision of more satisfactory services and assistance to these students.

Navarro and Shoemaker (2000) studied student performance and the perception of distance learners in cyberspace in terms of their attitude towards the essential instructional technologies, their perception towards the learner–instructor and learner–learner interactions, their satisfaction and related technical problems. They discovered that students preferred the cyberspace mode of learning, as the instructional technology could stimulate the classroom experience, support collaborative learning and interactive feedback. The support made available for student– student interaction via the electronic bulletin board enabled stimulating thoughts and debates to take place and led to satisfying and effective learning experiences.

The delivery model of the distance education academic programme at the School of Distance Education, University Saints Malaysia is comprised of the pedagogically articulated self-learning printed-text called modules which include the core teaching materials, video-conferencing teletutorials (scheduled), an annual residential intensive course and a five-day residential orientation programme in the main campus (Idrus and Zin, 1992).

Selected courses are also enriched by the use of audio and video tapes and the printed study guide. Based on this backdrop, the on-line learning environment is introduced for a more comprehensive learning experience.

Parameters for the Successful ICT Implementation

ICTs are swiftly evolving technologies, however, and so even the most ICT fluent teachers need to continuously upgrade their skills and keep abreast of the latest developments and best practices.

Research on the use of ICTs in different educational settings over the years invariably identify as a barrier to success the inability of teachers to understand why they should use ICTs and how exactly they can use ICTs to help them teach better. Unfortunately, most teacher professional development in ICTs is heavy on "teaching the tools" and light on "using the tools to teach."

Education Administrators

Leadership plays a key role in ICT integration in education. For

ICT integration programs to be effective and sustainable, administrators themselves must be competent in the use of the technology, and they must have a broad understanding of the technical, curricular, administrative, financial, and social dimensions of ICT use in education.

Technical Support Specialists

While the technical support requirements of an institution depend ultimately on what and how technology is deployed and used, general competencies that are required would be in the installation, operation, and maintenance of technical equipment (including software), network administration, and network security. Without on-site technical support, much time and money may be lost due to technical breakdowns.

Content Developers

Content development is a critical area that is too often overlooked. There is a need to develop original educational content (e.g., radio programs, interactive multimedia learning materials on CD-ROM or DVD, Web-based courses, etc.), adapt existing content, and convert print-based content to digital media. These are tasks for which content development specialists such as instructional designers, scriptwriters, audio and video production specialists, programmers, multimedia course authors, and web-developers are needed. Many universities with distance education programs, and those who otherwise make use of ICTs, have dedicated technical support and content development units.

Even in countries where English is a second language it is imperative that teaching and learning materials that match national curriculum requirements and have locally meaningful content, preferably in the local languages, be developed.

Technology and Distance learner support

Distance and open education schemes that have until recently relied mainly on the mailing of written materials, videos, cassette recordings, and radio or TV broadcasting techniques can be augmented, enhanced or replaced by new on-line tools and technologies which have the power to transform the learning environment.

Technological developments are coming together which offer the following benefits:

1. Through the Internet and worldwide web, new and enlarged sources of information and knowledge that offer teachers and students opportunities for self-development as well as benefits from incorporation into classroom environments.
2. Through e-mail and other Internet related feedback mechanisms, greater opportunity to reduce the isolation and time delay associated with distance education.
3. Through the extraordinary pace of software development, enriched teaching and learning with enhanced graphics, interaction, animation and visualisation.
4. Through lowering telecommunications bandwidth costs and emergence of enhanced cable, wireless and satellite systems 2G and 3G communications, greater opportunities for basic access, video conferencing, on-line interactive learning, and live interaction with the central place of a distance education programme.
5. Through community access schemes, more potential to make the benefits of distance education eventually available to lower income people and rural communities.

Sound pedagogical principles would increasingly dictate the need for a more interactive learning environment which was earlier difficult to achieve and also adds considerably to the remotest areas. But it was noted that its deployment requires expensive satellite resources as well as an expensive face-to-face lecture and broadcast system running in parallel.

Very Small Aperture Terminal (VSAT) satellite systems are increasingly seen as a powerful distribution mechanism for Internet based resources, with ready access to interactive learning tools and e-mail, especially when linked or packaged with key educational website sources, servers and services. VSATs can overcome many of the bandwidth/delivery speed, limitations of terrestrial systems, particularly in developing countries, and can be especially economic when deployed in an asymmetric multi-casting mode in which high-speed 'downlink' capability is combined with slower speed 'uplinking.'

These features and emerges the need of specially designed Distance Education network management and learner software packages of ICTs in distance education especially in the developing world.

Distance Education can be developed very well through Web based learning obviously, in Web-based learning; technical standardization of content has also become a pressing issue. Standardization allows different applications to share content and learning systems. Specifications in content, structure, and test formats are proposed so that interoperability may exist between different management systems, resulting in some cost-efficiencies. Standards must be general enough to support all kinds of learning systems and content. The ease by which Web-based educational content can be stored, transmitted, duplicated, and modified has also raised concerns about the protection of intellectual property rights.

The United Nations International World Intellectual Property Organization is leading international efforts in setting global standards for the protection of intellectual property rights that would not at the same time unduly curtail the accessing and sharing of information. For teachers and students, each of whom are potential publishers of multimedia materials that incorporate the works of others, information and training about the ethical use of intellectual property should be an important component of ICT-based programs.

Conclusion

Since communication and dialogue are at the heart of teaching and learning, technologies that facilitate the process over a network, particularly for learners distant from each other and the teacher are probably the most important. O'Malley has given an outline of Computer-supported collaborative learning (CSCL) technologies of which there are several types. The essential functions of CSCL for teaching and learning include one-to one much communication and the ability to work collaboratively in groups. Another facet of this mode of communication is that it may be synchronous or asynchronous.

Teaching and learning over a network (on-line) has resulted in changes in the roles and behaviour of teacher and student. It seems that students may become more involved in the learning process and that the authority of the teacher can be lessened.

The most useful function of the web from an educational view is that it can be used effectively as communication medium for student collaboration, an information resource, a search tool and as a medium for publication.

References

1. Distance Education at a Glance: Guide #6 – Computers in Distance Education, College of Engineering, University of Idaho, http://www.uidaho.edu/evo/ dist6.html; Jun 2001
2. Information Technology Policy for the Public Service, Ministry of Public Administration and Information, Republic of Trinidad and Tobago.
3. Jung, I (2001) Building a theoretical framework of web-based instruction in the context of distance education, *British Journal of Educational Technology* 32, 5, 525–534.
4. Klien, K. and Sorra, J. (1996), 'The Challenge of Innovation Implementation', Academy of Management Review, volume 21, number 4, pp.1055-1080.

5. Milheim, W (2001) Faculty and administrative strategies for effective implementation of distance education, *British Journal of Educational Technology,* 32, 5, 535–542.

6. Navarro, P and Shoemaker, J (2000) Performance and perception of distance learners in cyberspace, *The American Journal of Distance Education,* 14, 2, 15–35.

7. Shuell, JT and Farber, LS (2001) Students perceptions of technology use in college courses, *Journal of Educational Computing Research,* 24, 2, 119–138.

8. Thorpe, M. (2002). From independent learning to collaborative learning: New communities of practice in open, distance and distributed learning. In M. R. Lea & K. Nicoll (Eds.), *Distributed learning: Social and cultural approaches to practice* (pp. 131–151). London: RoutledgeFalmer.

26

The Factors Affecting the Quality in Distance Education

Introduction

This is provides decision makers with 32 trends that affect distance learning The trends are organized into categories as they pertain to students and enrollment, faculty members, academics, technology, the economy, and distance learning. All the trends were identified during an extensive in the field.

Major influences complicate the issue, such as the rapid advancement of technology, shifts in higher education audiences and learner profiles, faculty members' reactions, adapting campus cultures, and unsettled tensions between administrators, faculty members, and distance learning leaders. While identifying trends does not offer solutions to distance-learning challenges, decision makers will benefit by carefully considering each trend as it affects institution and goals. Themes emerged as the analysis progressed regarding students and enrollment, faculty members, academics, technology, the economy, and distance learning.

Student/Enrollment Trends

1. The current higher education infrastructure cannot accommodate the growing college-aged population and enrollments, making more distance education programs necessary.

Growth in college-age population and enrollments and the need for more lifelong learning for adults, many institutions acknowledge that within the decade there will be more students than their facilities can accommodate

2. Students *are shopping for courses that meet their schedules and circumstances*

More and more learners are requiring flexibility in program structure to accommodate their other responsibilities, such as full-time jobs or family needs .These constraints, students shop for courses that best accommodate their schedules and learning styles. Governors identified "allowing students to obtain education anytime and anyplace via technology" in the twenty-first century.

3. *Higher-education learner profiles, including online, information-age, and adult learners, are changing.*

Online students are becoming an entirely new subpopulation of higher-education learners. The modern, traditional-age college students are unlike past generations. They are "interested in small modules and short programs ... and in learning that can be done at home and fitted around work, family, and social obligations". Information-age learners prefer doing to knowing, trial-and-error to logic, and typing to handwriting.

Modern literacy includes not only text but also image and screen literacy. Today's adult learners differ still from traditional college-age students. They tend to be practical problem solvers. Their life experiences make them autonomous, self-directed, and goal- and relevancy-oriented. They are motivated by professional advancement, external expectations, the need to better serve others, social relationships, escape or stimulation, and pure interest in the subject.

4. the percentage of adult, female, and minority learners are increasing.

Growth in adult learners, women and minority learners is increasing.

5. Retention rates concern administrators and faculty members.

Studies comparing online course retention rates with traditional courses are inconclusive. But anecdotal evidence and studies by individual institutions suggest that course-completion and program-retention rates are generally lower in distance-education courses than in their face-to-face counterparts. "Many online students who drop a class may do so because it is the 'right thing' to do. Because of the requirements of school, work, and family life in general, students can benefit more from a class.

Faculty Trends

6. Traditional faculty roles are shifting or "unbundling.

"Distance education teams include administrators, instructional designers, technologists, and instructors. The functions of instructors "facilitator, teacher, organizer, grader, mentor, role model, counselor, coach, supervisor, problem solver, and liaison". The faculty in distance education requires "some specialized skills and strategies. Distance faculty members must be experts in maintaining communication, because there is increased demand for student interaction in distance learning.

7. They need for faculty development, support, and training is growing:

Faculty members tend initially to try to use their conventional classroom methods to teach at a distance and then become frustrated when attempts are unsuccessful.

8. Faculty tenure is being challenged, allowing for more non-traditional faculty roles in distance education.

Faculty tenure status is coming under more fire as new state, private, and for-profit distance-learning universities are created.

9. Some faculty members are resisting technological course delivery

Many faculty members will be reluctant to participate in online courses .They have some reason (i.e.) labor-intensive and time-consuming

10. *Faculty members who participate in distance education courses develop better attitudes toward distance education and technology.*

11. Instructors of distance courses can feel isolated.

This isolation may affect instructor satisfaction, motivation, and potential long-term involvement in distance learning".

12. Faculty members demand reduced workload and increased compensation for distance courses.

Most faculty members do spend more time on their distance courses.

Academic Trends

13. Knowledge and information are growing exponentially.

Knowledge proliferation may increase content-breadth.

14. The institutional landscape of higher education is changing: traditional campuses are declining, for-profit institutions are growing and public and private institutions are merging.

Profit institutions are the fastest-growing sector in education". Practice as "picking the low hanging fruit" by offering the more marketable courses, e.g., business, computer science, etc., and leaving the "heavy lifting" type of courses to traditional academe.

15. There is a shift in organizational structure toward decentralization.

Much of distance education programs' success or failure can be attributed to how it is organized. "The organization of CE [continuing education] is tended to be related to issues of centralization/ decentralization.

16. Instruction is becoming more learner-centered, non-linear, and self-directed.

Instructional approaches are becoming more learner-centered: "recursive and non-linear, engaging, self-directed, and meaningful from the learner's perspective. A pedagogical shift is likewise occurring within distance education, moving from a transmission model to constructivist, sociocultural and meta-cognitive models.

17. There is a growing emphasis on academic accountability.

In a recent poll by the North Central Association of Colleges and Schools, university presidents, administrators, and faculty members rated increasing demands for accountability.

18. A.cademic emphasis is shifting from course-completion to competency.

"Theoretical" and "seat-based time" to "outcomes-based" or "employer-based" competency.

19. Education is becoming more seamless between high school, college, and further studies.

As universities shift toward competency and institutions cater more closely to learners' specific needs.

20. Higher education outsourcing and partnerships are increasing.

Distance learning institutions are creating partnerships with other colleges, universities, companies, and other kinds of institutions to share technology and to produce and deliver courses. Winning accreditation, providing student services, setting tuition, figuring out finances, and transferring course credits are among the thorny issues.

21. Some advocate standardizing content in learning objects.

"The central issue in courseware development at the moment is the potential for developing reusable learning objects.

Technology Trends

22. Technological devices are becoming more versatile and ubiquitous

One of the most apparent trends affecting distance education is the advancement of technology. Infrastructures are growing stronger as computers double in speed while decreasing in cost, and high-speed network connections continue to expand. Computer, fax, picture phone, duplication, and other modalities are merging and becoming available at ever cheaper prices. The changes caused by broader use of e-texts. Videoconferencing and other technologies will also help enrich distance media and provide many benefits of face-to-face instruction.

23. There is a huge growth in Internet usage.

Not only is technology becoming more ubiquitous, it is being used more competently by more people from all nationalities, age groups, and socioeconomic levels.

24. Technological fluency is becoming a graduation requirement.

Universities are beginning to encourage students to take online courses, and even requiring students to take at least one online course before they graduate.

Economic Trends

25. with the economy in recession, there are fewer resources for higher education and higher education, initiatives, such as distance education.

26. Funding challenges are the top IT concern for many.

"The cost per student of a high-quality online learning program is the same as or greater than the per-student cost of physical school [i.e., traditional] education".

27. Lifelong learning is becoming a competitive necessity.

"The opportunity for training is becoming one of the most desirable benefits any job can offer".

Distance Learning Trends

28. More courses, degrees, and universities are becoming available through distance-education programs.

The literature is replete with evidence of the growing demand for distance education. Another factor influencing growth may be competition with other institutions.

29. The Internet is becoming dominant among other distance-education media.

"Today's distance education focus has dramatically shifted toward network-based technologies .Today, the Internet is being used more than other continuing education delivery strategies, such as ITV, correspondence, and live-remote location combinations. One reason for the growth is digital media are transferable, storable, and widely accessible.

30. The distinction between distance and local education is disappearing.

As universities digitally enhance more courses, the distinction between distance and local education is becoming blurred. "Even in a conventional 'face-to-face' system, students spend much of their time working on their own. But the increase in resources for individual learning.

31. The need for effective course-management systems and Web services is growing.

All the growth in online education, student- and course-managing systems are becoming ever more crucial.

32. ***There is an increasing need for learning and teaching strategies that exploit the capabilities of technology.***

Technological advancements have naturally caused distance educators to ask how "new technologies such as wireless, mobile laptop computing, personal digital assistants (PDAs), videoconferencing, video streaming, virtual reality, and gaming environments enhance distributed learning.

Conclusion

Many trends in higher education will influence the future of distance learning. Student enrollments are growing to surpass the capacity of traditional infrastructures, learner profiles are changing, and students are shopping for education that meets their needs. Traditional faculty roles, motivation, and training needs are shifting while workload, compensation, and instructional issues continue to deter them from distance learning participation. The Internet and other information technology devices are becoming more ubiquitous while technological fluency is becoming a common expectation. Institutions will strengthen their distance-learning strategic plans by identifying and understanding distance-education trends for student enrollments, faculty support, and larger academic, technological and economic issues.

27

Distance Education: Learner Centred Education

Distance Education

The idea that it is possible to learn, outside, the traditional classroom, the concept of .breaking down the walls of the schoolhouse, and opening education to greater numbers of people, of various ages and condition who are widely dispersed, are notions that did not spring to life with the revolution in technology that occurred with the development of the computer or the Internet Rather, these are ideas that have held great appeal, one could argue, for more than a century, and can be traced back to Sir Isaac Pittman, who not only invented shorthand, but also hit upon the brilliant idea of providing instruction to a potentially limitless audience through correspondence courses delivered by mail. In the nineteenth century, correspondence courses were available to students in Britain, Germany, Japan and the United States, and by the twentieth century they formed a significant part of the educational offerings in the most advanced countries (Matthews 1999).

The Range Of Experiences

Bearing in mind its lengthy history, it is not surprising that the term distance education should be used to cover a wide range of different experiences. Winthrop Carty defines it as all education that delivers training and information between two or more places regardless of whether that education is:

1. **Synchronous.** Using same-time communications; usually interactive, as in Internet chats or interactive videoconferencing.

2. **Asynchronous.** Communications that do not require participants to exchange information at the same time, such as e-mail or mail correspondence.

3. **One-way**. Information delivered from one point to one or many other points with no response capability, such as television broadcasting.

4. **Two-way**. Any communication in which the flow is bi-directional, implying but not limited to synchronous, interactive communication.

5. **Multi-point**. Information delivered simultaneously from one place to many other places, as in videoconferencing from one classroom to several other remote classrooms.

6. **Multi-cast**. Usually consisting of transmission of a video or audio clip to the computers of many users (Carty 1999).

Learner Centred Principles in Distance Education

In order to assist in the reform of education, the American Psychological Association (APA) formed a task force to design new strategies for the improvement of teaching and learning. The APA formed the Learner-Centered Principles (LCP), which provide a framework for developing curriculum that emphasizes active and reflective learning. LCP integrates social constructivist and cognitive theories, as well as motivational and individual differences. LCP curriculum should emphasize the incorporation of the needs, skills, interests and backgrounds of the learners. The goal of LCP is to provide active and collaborative learning environments.

Learner Centered Environments should:

a) Challenge students
b) Provide an explanation of what is expected
c) Give the learners choices and control
d) Encourage learners to work cooperatively
e) Allow learners to feel respected and valued for their opinions
f) Provide individualized attention to personal learning preferences
g) Allow learners input into what standards and methods will be used for evaluation

There are fourteen Learner-Centered Principles, which are divided into four domains.

1. Cognitive and Meta-cognitive Factors
   a) Nature of the learning process
   b) Goals of the learning process
   c) Construction of knowledge
   d) Strategic thinking
   e) Thinking about thinking
   f) Context of learning
2. Motivational and Affective Factors
   a) Motivational and emotional influences on learning
   b) Intrinsic motivation to learn
   c) Effects of motivation on effort
3. Developmental and Social Factors
   a) Developmental influences on learning
   b) Social influences on learning

4. Individual Differences
   a) Individual differences in learning
   b) Learning and diversity
   c) Standards and assessment

Transactional Mode of Distance Education

Distance Education (DE) is a form of teaching where the student is not required to be physically present at a specific location, such as in the case of online classes and telecourses.

As a result of the lack of face-to-face contact, instructors are strongly encouraged to develop strategies and instruction that leads to high interaction, such as, communication, participation and feedback. The American Distance Education Consortium (ADEC) provides outlines with guiding principles that can be used in developing DE curriculum. These principles include the importance of designing active and effective learning and providing support to the needs of the learners (ADEC).

According to McIssac&Gunawardena, there is not a single formulated theory for DE. However, there are four theoretical frameworks that have provided a deeper understanding for DE: Transactional Distance, Interactivity Theory, Social Context, and Control (Distance Education Theory).

Transactional Distance: location does not determine the effect on instruction. It is, however, the interaction between the student and the instruction that determines the distance. Distance is determined by the relationship between dialog (interaction/ relationship between learner and instructor) and class structure (learning objective, instruction, etc), and not by the physical distance between the learner and instructor. More structure and fewer dialogs contribute to a greater distance.

Interactivity Theory: there are three types of relations in instructions.

a) Learner/Instructor: The interaction between the student and the teacher. The instructor should be the facilitator of knowledge and provide feedback, support and encouragement to the student.

b) Learner/Context: The manner how the student obtains the information. Learner should be given the content so that they can construct their own understanding.

c) Learner/Learner: The exchange of ideas between the students. DE interaction supports the development of community building.

Social Context: This is how the environment effects motivation, attitudes, teaching and learning.

Control: This is how students view his/her role in learning. This requires a balance of the learner's independence, competence (ability and skill), and support (both human and material).

Advantages of Distance Education

A great many potential benefits for distance learners in both developed and developing countries are cited in the literature. Principal among these is the greater access to education that distance learning offers, above all to what is increasingly referred to as the non-traditional student generally a person who is not 18 to 25 years old and not able to attend a conventional in-class university course. In this regard, the flexibility of scheduling, the possibility of proceeding at one own pace, the opportunity to study without having to travel, indeed without leaving home, and in the best funded programmes, the individualized attention from the instructor are attractive features of distance education that win praise from students and educators.

In addition, for institutions that manages to persuade or oblige instructors to bring their course online the opportunity to reach distance students holds out the hope of great savings in the construction of classroom buildings, student housing, parking lots and other physical infrastructure, as well as substantial potential savings in teaching salaries. Moreover, mounting such a programme benefits an institution because it requires the university to keep abreast of new technology, and signals the public that the institution is forward thinking and technologically advanced.

Benefits of Extending Distance Education to the Developing World

With government funding more limited and university education more costly, developing countries cannot rely, as in the past, on sending the best and the brightest, or even the richest, abroad for training so that this educated elite can serve as a conduit of knowledge from the industrialized to the developing world. In the face of the pressure on developing countries to join the global information economy or perish many express the hope that distance education will provide the opportunity to train more people better and at lower cost (Carty 1999).

Conclusion

For the most part Distance Education is simply education at a distance with common frameworks based on learner-centered principles. DE integrates the use of interactive, multimedia technologies to enhance individual learning. Additionally the role of the instructor in DE is more of a facilitator providing the source of content and resources. Lastly DE encourages individuals to become their own knowledge navigators, taking control of their education.

Resources

1. McIsaac, M.S. &Gunawardena, C.N. (1996) Distance Education Theory. Retrieved October 5, 20005, from http://seamonkey.ed.asu.edu/~mcisaac/dechapter/theory.htm.
2. About ADEC, Background on the American Distance Education Consortium, http://www.adec.edu/admin/adec-background.html

3. Learner-Centered Psychological Principles: A Framework for School Redesign and Reform http://www.apa.org/ed/lcp.html

4. Thomas, J. (Spring 2003) Learner-Centred teaching: postsecondary strategies that promote thinking like a professional. Retrieved October 13, 2005, from http://www.findarticles.com/p/articles/mi_m0NQM/is_2_42/ai_102696729

5. Chou, C. (2004) A model of learner-centred computer-mediated interaction for collaborative distance education. *International Journal of E-Learning, 3*(1), 11.

6. McCombs, B &Vakili, D. (2005) A learner-centred framework for e-learning. *Teachers College Record, 107(*8), 1582-1609.

28

English Language in the Digital Age

Introduction

Online English Education is likely to co-exist with other Communication technologies and modes of imparting and acquiring knowledge skills of language and value based systems. With easy availability and accessibility of computer hardware, the online mode of language learning would carve a niche for itself in both conventional and Open Distance learning (ODL) Systems. The need of the hour is to build sound infrastructure and provide basic amenities particularly in rural and Semi-urban areas for the success of Online-language learning.

Role of English Teachers

Excellent teachers in English are a rare resource all over the world. This concept is true in the digitally divided communities. Some teachers have a wrong notion that an increased use of information and communication Technologies (ICTs) would replace their image in the mind of the students, as Online English Teaching is being planned more systematically than the routine preparation by them.

To overcome this barrier English Teachers need to be trained on different aspects of online learning to enhance their skills. Teachers can integrate audio, video graphics and text to highlight what they are trying to teach. English teachers should be motivated to use digital resources such as Online and Offline multimedia course ware, laboratory, library etc., more language trainers are seen to adopt new technologies for communication, business and Educational purposes.

Role of Mobile

Mobile Technology is expected to reduce the urban-rural digital divide in the country. Voice services, data access and learners of English language can exchange information with teachers through a variety of Information and Communication Technologies. This can enable the language learners to gain control of the learning process and achieve mastery in given topic. Admissions and examinations can also be made flexible to suit the needs of the language learners through this Digital mode of learning. English language learners have to be technologically literate and acquire necessary skills to use computer devices for storage, dissemination and retrieval of information as and when required.

Among the various modes of English learning, online learning in India is becoming a need of the hour. Language learners can make use of Internet service providers for reading the content, searching information, watching video, playing games, reviewing research literature, conducting financial Transactions etc., Internet Service providers will help thousands of language students to exchange and share their views, doubts, problems etc., relating to the their study.

Digital user

Digital users aim to make use of new methods and media for English teaching and learning by focusing on correct pedagogy for Online Education, providing facilities for experiments through virtual lab and Online Testing and Certification. Learning, discovery and creative expressions are fundamental things in the language teaching.

Online Learning

Online English learning is an opportunity as well as a challenge. There are mainly two components. (1) Generation of E-Content and (2) Connectivity for Institutions and learners. If the Connectivity is in place, the cost of E-devices comes down. Then the penetration of broad band would reach and rural and remote areas. It would bridge the digital divide and the gap in the skills to use and computing devices for teaching and learning among rural and urban Teachers and students. India spent a lot of money and Time on expanding the reach, access and overall quantity of students. Yet plenty needs to be done on the quality aspect. Video downloads are being used in urban India, while basic voice services in the rural area are far from satisfactory. Edusat network provides two-way communication (video & audio) between the teachers at the studio and the children in the remote schools. To achieve this goal language teachers should be encouraged to make a shift in their teaching-learning strategies by adopting ICT enabled situations.

Access, inclusion and Excellence are the three pillars of English Education. These pillars would become strong through online learning. The need of the hour is to provide good quality in English learning and make the language more relevant to the emerging needs of the society. Educators should create quality, equity and equality in English language learning when they teach to their students.

Most of the online courses are available in English and a large Section of Society including the general Public and Students find it difficult to communicate in English. New courses are being made available in Indian languages. Greater efforts need to be made in designing and developing quality courses in Indian languages.

Challenges Facing the Digital Age

1. English language Domination

2. Educational System Inertia.
3. Relevant Content.
4. Instructional Design.
5. Digital Gap.
6. Mindset.
7. Lack of research support.
8. High cost of technology.
9. Re-Organise the curriculum.
10. Constant Power Supply.

Conclusion

The Advantages of Online learning need to be viewed with Caution. Younger generation is using new Information and communication Technologies (ICTs) and its tools, collaborative sites and blogs, platforms like face book and twitter, video-conferencing and mobile Technologies in a big way. Teachers need to master these techniques by learning to teach in virtual learning environment play the role of a facilitator and provide greater control of learning to the students for lifelong learning.

29

Technical Education in Distance Mode

Technical education

In recent times very little attention has been paid to the historical context of our current quandaries/dilemmas over technical education and training. It will hopefully provide a host of insights into this country's current struggle to confront and tackle skills shortages and our ability to respond to and compete with the emerging global economies. It will provide pointers to the lessons and strategies for technical education aimed at industrial growth that have been spelt out over the last 200+ years but which successive governments and educationalists have continued to neglect or discard.

In addition to the contributions to science and technology across the home countries I am also acutely aware of the contributions made from further afield both within Europe and beyond. One only has to read the seminal works of Joseph Needham on the history of Chinese science and technology to realize the significant contributions that this civilization made to these important bodies of knowledge. China made an immense number of discoveries and inventions centuries before the European countries including gunpowder, the magnetic compass and printing.

A remaining mystery is why China did not continue to build on these amazing achievements. One must also remember the massive achievements to mathematics, science and technology made by the Middle Eastern countries and civilizations and the Greek and Roman empires. Also the Muslim civilizations preserved, recorded and translated key works in mathematics, science, technology for future generations as well as adding further to many of the subjects.

Importance of technical education

Education is important for every individual in a nation. It plays a vital role to change the stare of a country. Basically, Education is divided into three groups. The Education which teaches the concerns of a society is called Social Education. The Education which develops a personality inside a man himself is called Spiritual Education. The Education that concerns with the professionalism is called Vocational Education. The Technical Education comes under the branch of Vocational Education which deals practically in the field of trade, commerce, agriculture, medicine & Engineering.

We are living in the modern age of science where we found Technologies in every aspect of life. What makes life so brain friendly for us simply; these are the Technologies which we use for our ease and comforts. Not only in our daily life but also in the research centre, in defensive measured of a country, biological aspects etc. Using a technology is far easier than to develop it. For developing a technology, it needed high skill teams which have a high data for the theme. It also needed a high amount of time and also money.

Technical education in regular mode

- Universities / institutions shall frame ordinances / regulations / rules, as the case may be, spelling out the outline of the programmes to be offered through the regular mode indicating the number of required credits, list of courses with assigned credits, reading references in addition to self-learning material, hours of study, contact classes at study centres, assignments, examination and evaluation process, grading etc.

- UGC shall only assess the competence of university/ institute in respect of conducting regular education programmes by a team of experts, whose report shall be placed before the Council of UGC for consideration.
- The approval shall be given only after consideration by Council of UGC and not by Chairperson, UGC. For the purpose, minimum number of mandatory meetings of UGC may be prescribed.
- AICTE would be directed under section 20 (1) of AICTE Act 1987 to ensure accreditation of the programmes in Computer Sciences, Information Technology and Management proposed to be offered by an institute/ university through the regular mode, by National Board of Accreditation (NBA). And it also insists the accreditation as very important aspect to institutions.

Technical education in distance mode

Technical education, also known as vocational education, prepares students for jobs related to a particular trade, often involving manual or practical activities. The learner develops skills or expertise for a certain trade or job, through participation, to discover the actual work surrounding it. With the rising number of high school drop outs, technical education has become a source to earn a living from, in order to train for a specific job.

Technical jobs used to be considered the 'poor man's' job but due to diversification many jobs we consider essential to the smooth operation of a country or facilities rely on technical staff. This category of education may be classified as procedural knowledge. Usually individuals with at least a secondary or at times primary education are eligible to receive technical instruction in order to further their career ambitions in a particular job.

In this day and age, nurses, auto technicians and mechanics, welders, blacksmiths, tailors, repair men, bakers, chefs and industries like Applied Science; Business Administration; Child Education and Community Services; Construction; Design; Printing, Textiles and Clothing; Hotel, Service and Tourism Studies; Information Technology; Electrical and Electronic Engineering; and Mechanical, Manufacturing and Industrial Engineering. As well as traditional crafts and cottage industries all fall under technical education. Almost every country caters for such education through institutes, community colleges and universities to better equip their population with this vital know how, critical to the operation of a country. Usually a certain amount of education is required to take up a technical course. At least primary leading on to secondary education is necessary, to ensure the student can read, write and to an extent solve math problems which include measurement and money matters. Most courses begin from 3 months to 2 years depending on the path chosen by the student. Very little material is in the form of learning material and text books. The majority of the course stretches over a hands on approach regarding 'how' to do certain things. The instructors or technicians teaching these courses are well versed experts with years of on hand experience. The student therefore learns from the best possible teaching staff concerning their area of study. Besides this, they are inculcated with proficiency which enables them to tackle new problems, as well refresher courses, which inform them of the latest innovative technologies making their profession less complicated. Technically educated individuals or skilled workers earn a first-rate living due to the fact that their specialties are always sought. For people intending to migrate abroad, most countries offer superior benefits for skilled work force, making it an excellent earning opportunity for experts.

Skilled workers have their fair share of problems due to the advancement of technology. Nonetheless, a well selected skilled profession can never go out of demand. With the recent recession, technically educated individuals are the least effected due to the ever rising requirement of their expertise.

Technical education in India

The history of imparting formal technical education in India can be traced back to mid-19th century, although it got momentum in 20th century with the setup of Constitution of Technical Education Committee of the Central University Board of Education (CUBE) in 1943; Preparation of Sergeant Report in 1944 and Formation of All India Council of technical Education (AICTE) in 1945. With the country gaining independence in 1947, the development of technical education had become a major concern for the government of India to face the new challenges and move the country forward.

The setup of Indian Institutes of Technology, Indian Institutes of Management and Indian Institutes of Science was a major step in the development of technical education in the country. The quality of education of these institutes have managed to change the outlook of India so much that this ancient country which was earlier known for yoga and meditation is now known for computer engineers. However, it does not mean that the challenge of making technical education accessible to the rural populace and other under developed sections of the society has been overcome.

In order to maintain the standard of technical education, a statutory authority- the All India Council for Technical Education (AICTE) - was set up in 1945. AICTE is responsible for planning, formulation and maintenance of norms and standards, quality assurance through accreditation, funding in priority areas, monitoring and evaluation, maintaining parity of certification and awards and ensuring coordinated and integrated development and management of technical education in the country.

Technical Education Courses in India: The courses, which are known as 'technical' in India and therefore come under the purview of All India Council of Technical Education are - degree and diploma courses in Engineering, Master degree Courses in Engineering, Master of Computer Application (MCA), Master of Business Administration (MBA), Pharmacy Courses, Courses in Architecture and Applied Arts and Hotel Management and Catering Technology Courses.

Difficulties in teaching technical education in distance education:

Student Barriers to Distance Learning

Problems and barriers encountered by the student fall into several distinct categories; costs and motivators, feedback and teacher contact, student support and services, alienation and isolation, lack of experience, and training. A second area of concern for the distance student is the perceived lack of feedback or contact with the teacher. Because there is not daily or weekly face to face contact with teachers, students may have trouble in self-evaluation.

These barriers can be mitigated through technological methods such as e-mail. Computer conferencing and electronic mail can be integrated into the delivery of the course to provide the missing interactivity. Because both are essentially asynchronous, they continue to leave the student in charge of setting his or her own work times — a critical success factor for the distance student. It is important that the student receive prompt feedback in any institutional setting, particularly in distance learning where the learner is impaired by the lack of casual contact with the teacher and other students. This is especially important for those students who live outside metropolitan areas. They may not have access to reliable telecommunications, computers, and postal mail. The frustrations resulting from problems with communication between student and academic institution are factors of which distance education planners should be well aware (Wood, 1996).

A third area of concern for distance students is the lack of support and services such as providing tutors, academic planners and schedulers, and technical assistance. The isolation that results from the distance learning process can complicate the learning process for adult students. Support for distance learners should not be overlooked when planning distance programs. Students need tutors and academic planners to help those complete courses on time and to act as a support system when stress becomes a problem. Planners from Washington State University (WSU) note that "student services are a significant part of the budgeted costs of the program." They also believe that "success in attracting, serving, and retaining students will hinge more on excellent student support services than on any technology issues." (Oaks, 1996). Technology costs and considerations can be a source of budgeting problems; however, student support for distance learners should take precedence.

A fourth problem area is the feelings of alienation and isolation reported by distance students. Students of all kinds want to be part of a larger school community, and simply a member of a "correspondence" course. For many traditional students, this is an important part of their social lives.

If students are undertaking distance learning courses that require knowledge of computers, then the students must be taught, at a minimum, the fundamentals of operating the system of choice of the distance-taught course. If distance learning is to be successful, technical barriers must be made a non-issue.

Faculty Barriers in Distance Learning

Faculty experience problems such as lack of staff training in course development and technology, lack of support for distance learning in general, and inadequate faculty selection for distance learning courses. Sometimes the coursework for traditional and distance students is the same. Often it is not. There can be a lot of up front effort in designing distance learning material. This can impose a burden on teachers who already have material for traditional classrooms. Computers, video equipment, communications software, and the like, present challenges and frustrations. Faculty must know how to the use these technologies if they are to teach distance courses. Training students and staff, particularly in troubleshooting problems, is imperative to success in technical distance learning.

Teachers may lack the basic skills or hardware to fully participate in distance education. The advent of computers, telecommunications, and the World Wide Web provides an unprecedented opportunity for faculty and students to learn in a cooperative environment. It is interesting to note, however, that students respond to this changing environment more adeptly than teachers do. At California State University, for example, more than 50% of the student body own home computers while less than 50% of the faculty (Syllabus Magazine, 1996). Obtaining proper equipment and training is critical in teacher acceptance of distance learning.

Another problem perceived by faculty is the threat to tenure and human resource staffing. Depending on the school and the academic department, courses taught as part of a distance program may not always count toward tenure considerations, thus causing a disincentive for participation by some non-tenured faculty (Oaks, 1996). Additionally, if one professor can serve thousands of students there will obviously be fewer professors and fewer departments and faculties. Schools must not underestimate this resistance and should be very aware of the possibility of overburdening faculty and staff.

Teachers also have problems respecting the academics of distance courses. One way of enhancing commitment is by forcing distance courses through the same approval process as on-campus courses. One way to mitigate these potentially serious problems is by selecting teachers who are relatively senior people, good teachers, like the idea of distance learning and want to participate in it. Interest and motivation are not success factors reserved only for the student. Faculties who want to teach distance courses are certainly more likely to be successful than faculty that are forced to teach these courses.

Organizational Barriers in Distance Learning

Student and teacher concerns represent the human aspects of

distance programs. Organizational problems, especially infrastructure and technology problems, also present challenges. Faculties who teach distance education courses need organizational and administrative support from the institution. Funding should be provided to create an administrative unit that is to be responsible for managing the program. Institutional leaders must be committed to distance programs.

Technology considerations are self-evident but are the most easily solved. Technology problems include; financing new technology, telecommunications, hardware issues, course production and technology, and Internet problems.

A primary concern for both learning institutions and students is availability of funds. When technology is used, the costs increase substantially for both the student and the institution. Universities must consider the initial costs as well as the continuing costs of installing, maintaining, using, and upgrading technology to support distance services. Telecommunications and connectivity costs such as those needed to use the Internet, are ongoing costs.

Distance education via simultaneous two-way audio-visual interaction systems such as video teleconferencing, brings an additional set of issues to be considered by the instructor and effective models for this delivery system need to be identified (Sweet, 1986).

Some students, particularly those without home computers with modems could have difficulty communicating with the university or teacher. Lack of adequate hardware and the subsequent cost barrier of obtaining equipment could place undue hardship on some remote students. However, implementing other communications systems (phone mail, etc.) could help overcome this barrier.

Learning institutions must develop distance learning course material or pay a hefty price to order materials from distributors. For some institutions, the investment in production technology may be worth the cost; however, a significant investment is necessary for production facilities, equipment, and personnel to produce videotapes. Using the Internet instead can overcome some of this problem but it poses additional difficulties in insuring all students have adequate access to the Internet.

Solutions to Overcome Difficulties in Technical Education

In the past the differentiation between distance education and on campus studies has been obvious. Print based delivery for distance students and lectures, tutorials and practical sessions for on campus students. Now emerging educational technology provides opportunities to use enhanced learning materials that are interesting and educationally refined alternatives for the student who prefers to study via distance education.

However, as Sherry (1996) claims: "too often instructional designers and curriculum developers have become enamoured of the latest technologies without dealing with the underlying issues of learner characteristics and needs, the influence of media upon the instruction process, equity of access to interactive delivery systems, and the new roles of teacher, site facilitator, and student in the distance learning process."

The students are given more responsibility for their own learning and as a consequence, spend more time in self-directed learning sessions. Distance education is of course no longer limited to print based materials. Video, CD-ROM and Internet delivery are all viable options today. It is now conceivable that on-campus and distance students could end up studying in similar ways using the same media.

Technical education in the Future

In common with all sections of the community, technical teachers find the progress of the War marked by increasing demands upon them. Apart from special courses, the average experience appears to be of a large increase in the part-time day classes of the colleges and the maintenance of evening or the substituted week-end classes at something approaching their normal level. To cater for these with, in many cases, depleted staffs has called for sacrifices of many of our cherished ideas as to conditions of service-changes in hours of duty per week, sizes of classes and suitability of accommodation for classes-which will demand the watchful care of the Association if they are to be regarded as temporary expedients and not precedents.

The future lies in the technical education. It has to be relevant education; the very latest technology that is being developed should be part of the curriculum. We want to have more Gross Enrolment Ratio (GER) in technical education. For this we need to have more number of engineering colleges. We have formulated letter of approval (LOA) for this purpose. We are going for second shift in all government polytechnic colleges. The capacity of diploma holders will double as a result of this.

Regarding higher education, we want to add a lot of emphasis on value education. Quality of higher education is an area of concern. We will take care of the issue of filling up vacant issues. One more step to be taken is to have a uniform syllabus in all universities across the state. Training of teachers is also an important aspect, which is being looked into. Quality should be an integral and important aspect, which should be mentioned very categorically.

Conclusion

Given the importance of technical education in the further development of the nation. Those considering the negative aspects of distance learning say that the asynchronous nature of online education takes some getting used to, moreover conducting a seamless discussion might not be possible because it is performed at various levels and speeds at different places. If a student is not familiar with technology, he might find it difficult to follow a discussion. Delayed responses and pending messages may further hinder group performances. Another researcher DR Garrison in his research paper conclusion of distance learning states that though distance education through online means may be collaborative learning, the challenge lies in understanding the technology in order to apply it to create new and more effective learning situations.

References

1. *Chou, P.* (1994). Guide to managing a telecourse/distance learning program. Suisun, California: Learning Resources Association.
2. Cuskelly E Purnell K Lawrence G 1995 *Student Experiences of Distance Education at Central Queensland University: Findings from Focus Group Research* ISBN 1875902198
3. Holgate E 1997 *Extent of non-print media used for distance education at CQU in 1996.* DDCE seminar presentation September 1997.
4. Jones D 1996 Solving some problems of University Education: A Case Study in *Proceedings of AusWeb96* Southern Cross University Press Gold Coast Roger Debreceny Allan Ellis pp243-252
5. Jones D 1996 Computing by Distance Education: Problems and Solutions*Integrating Technology into Computer Science Education*Assocaition for Computing Machinery Barcelona Gordon Davies pp139 – 146
6. McCormack C Jones D 1997 *Building a Web-based Education System* John Wiley & Sons Sherry L 1996 Issues in Distance Learning in *International Journal of Distance Education*Vol 1 No 4 pp337-365

30

Factors Affecting the Development of Distance Education

Introduction

The idea of learning from others at a distance is by no means new. Some scholars claim that the epistles of St Paul sent to individual churches illustrate some key concepts of distance education. In 1840 Isaac Pitman started what is generally credited as the first correspondence course, offering tuition in shorthand by post to students in the United Kingdom. In Germany in the 1850s Gustav Langenscheidt published Lehrbriefe (literally, teaching letters) for language instruction by letter for adults to teach themselves. Opportunities to study at a distance at higher education level began with the foundation of the University of London in the United Kingdom in 1836. Students being taught in approved colleges and institutions elsewhere were allowed to take examinations conducted by the University. From 1858 the examinations were opened up for candidates from all over the world, regardless of how or where they had prepared for the examinations. This led to the setting up a number of correspondence colleges providing courses covering the curriculum specified by the University.

Various factors had a significant influence on the development of distance education. These included the pressure for expansion of higher education generally, the arrival of the second generation of distance education, and increased government expenditure. Other contributory factors were the changing nature of the workforce, with people looking for second-chance education or undertaking in-service education to improve their career prospects. Distance education seemed too many decision-makers to be the obvious solution.

Pressures for Expansion

The involvement of government in the active planning of higher education development is a relatively new phenomenon. Up till the middle of the 20th century, attention focused on the problems of securing expansion and universal participation in secondary education. This was mainly resolved in most (though not all) countries by the mid-1960s. New and important objectives of the 1960s were the extension of access to higher education, the move from opportunities for small elite to mass higher education, the extension of programmes of continuing education and the improvement of professional skills and training of specialists. Such major changes required innovative forms of delivery and provided the impetus for the founding of new, non-traditional forms of higher education institution.

During the 1960s policy makers were looking for ways and means of making education more democratic and professional. Distance education was a means of providing educational services to a large number of people who wanted to learn, but who were unable or unwilling to take time out for traditional forms of education. The didactic framework of higher education could be significantly enlarged by the addition of an alternative to traditional forms of education where learners could study independently within the control and supervision of higher education institutions.

Second Generation Distance Education

A major factor which helped to establish the status and quality of distance education was the creation of the Open University of the United Kingdom (UKOU) in 1969. This was important for the practice of distance education and a demonstration of the integration of media into the teaching process.

Later on government pressure and competition for students forced traditional institutions to review their structures, curricula and programmes, as well as forms and methods of education, and to consider the use of new technology and the development of distance learning programmes.

Increased Expenditure

Public pressure and practical need led to large increases in government expenditure on higher education in the 1960s and 1970s. The pressures for expansion and the demonstration of successful and large scale distance teaching through the establishment of the Open University of the U K meant that governments were willing to allocate money for setting up new institutions and for traditional institutions to expand and diversify their methods of teaching. Societal attitudes to education changed as well. Education was now regarded as a major contributory factor to economic growth and social development which could help to solve national and global problems. Both developed and developing countries saw education as a key to their future prosperity. While developed countries tried to maintain and strengthen their positions in the world market, developing countries hoped to bridge the gap in economic and social development.

Globalisation and economic competition between nations has led to rivalry in the sphere of science and technology and to the need for an educated workforce. Education is high on the list of priorities for investment, at both public and private level.

Three Generations of Distance Education

One way of looking at the history and successive developments in distance education has been to describe them as belonging to different 'generations'. Garrison (1985) and Nipper (1989) were among the first to use this term to describe three phases of distance education, 'which are linked historically to the development of production, distribution and communication technologies' (Nipper 1989 p. 63).

The medium for the first generation was written and printed material. While writing had been in use for centuries, the introduction of new printing techniques enabled low cost production of textbooks. From the middle of the nineteenth century the establishment of railway systems and fast and economical national postal services enabled the distribution of teaching materials to large numbers of geographically dispersed learners. In addition to generally available textbooks, specially developed instructional materials were limited and may have included a reading list and sample questions which were marked by correspondence tutors.

The invention of radio in the 1920's saw the beginning of radio-led courses consisting of a series of talks; occasionally a set book or other printed materials and local study groups were included. From the 1950's TV-led courses have been extensively used, often with print and local groups and occasionally student assessment.

The beginning of the second generation was marked by the setting up of the Open University of the U K in 1969- This was the first time that a deliberately integrated multiple media approach had been used for distance education, even though the dominant medium was still print. The Open University developed large quantities of high-quality, specially designed distance learning materials. One-way communication, from university to students, was through print integrated with broadcasts (audio cassettes were added later). Two-way communication, between tutors and students, was through correspondence tutoring, face-to-face tutorials and short residential schools. A characteristic of this model is high fixed costs associated with the development of courses, and low variable costs in that the cost of each additional student is low, once materials have been created.

The third generation of distance education uses information and communications technology as its basis, offering two-way communication in various forms (text, graphics, sound, moving pictures) either synchronous ('at the same time' as in videoconferencing and audio graphics, both popular in North American institutions) or asynchronous ('not at the same time' as in electronic mail, use of the Internet and computer conferencing). This technology can be added on to courses that are more characteristic of earlier generations, or it can be used by itself. In both cases it can facilitate greater interactivity between tutor and student, between student and student and between student and learning resource of various kinds. Discounting the initial costs of the technology, this model may generate lower up-front fixed costs, but higher variable (eg for the student) costs than the second generation model.

Conclusion

The history of distance education demonstrates its flexibility in responding to new educational needs and its relevance in many different countries around the world. As new technologies have become available, distance education has changed so that it is possible to refer to three generations. Pressure for educational expansion, including the need for continuing education, has led to increased expenditure and a willingness of governments to fund new methods. The creation of the U K O U as an autonomous university signalled the beginning of second generation high quality university level distance education, which offered a model taken up elsewhere. However, it represents only one model and there are others which provide alternative routes for the development of distance education.

References

1. Beeth, J. (1982) 'Distance Students' Learning - Empirical Findings and Theoretical Deliberations' in *Distance Education,* 3,(1), Pp. 6-27
2. Bates, A. W. (1991) *'Third Generation Distance Education: the Challenge of New Technology',*
3. Research in Distance Education, 3, (2), Pp. 10-15
4. Daniel, J.S. and Marquis, C. (1979) 'Interaction and Independence: Getting the Mixture Right' in *Teaching at a Distance,* 14 Pp. 29-44
5. Evans, T. and Nation, D . (1989) *'Dialogue in Practice,* Research and Theory in Distance Education' in Open Learning, 4, (2) Pp. 37- 42.
6. Garrison, D.R. (1985) 'Three generations of technological innovations in distance education', in *Distance Education,* 6, (2) Pp. 235-241.

31

Enhancing Student Support Services in Distance Education

Introduction

Education is considered to be the most forceful instrument of development. Therefore it must reach all people living in every nook and corner of the country. Distance education helps the economically weaker sections and the people who do not have time and money to spend in school, colleges and universities to receive education or to increase their academic qualification.

Concept of distance education

The concept of distance education has been universally accepted as an alternative to the institutional teaching to provide a second chance for providing higher education to those who missed the opportunity of getting the same at their normal stage. Distance education is innovative in the sense that it sets up its own norms, approaches, and methodology which are different from the face-to-face system of education. Today it has evolved into an independent system of education, thanks to the growth of communication technologies and the cognitive sciences which are flexible enough to use the technologies for pedagogic purposes.

Conventional Teaching

In the conventional classroom teaching, there is dialogue between the teacher and the learner which enhances confidence and self-learning among the learners. This interaction between the teacher and students makes the learning effective. The teacher can use a lot of strategies and skills to explain, demonstrate to provide academic as well as non-academic support to his/her students. The students also get opportunity to interact with their peer group, whereas, the distance learner is deprived of this situation. Secondly, the distance learners belong to heterogeneous group, in the sense that they differ in their age, interests, background, needs, and experiences.

Need for Student Support Service

Usually working personal or professionals go for distance education, aiming at higher degree or promotion. Hence, they are more mature with a lot of experiences. At the same time when we look at the learners in distance education now we understand that many discontinued their formal education for various reasons. Some of them may be school dropouts with an incomplete education. Hence their attitude towards learning is different from the regular students.

Since the formal face to face environment is lacking in distance education the learner has to depend on the well-designed written study material for learning. They do not have the opportunity of interacting frequently with the teachers. Hence, they may need assistance in solving the problems related to their study habits, time managements, motivation, and academic guidance etc. Because of the diversity of background and abilities to learn in isolation, distance education learners need support service at different times of their learning.

Characteristics of Course Material

In distance education system the face to face interaction, teaching in the classroom is replaced by specially designed self-learning materials or course materials. Since the self-learning material is well designed it gives the objectives of each unit in the beginning of the lesson itself. The material also gives the clear structure of the unit, carries number of exercises and activities for a learner to master familiarize the content.

Even though, the self-learning material is well defined and designed they need help from the teachers, since distance learners have different diverse background and learning skills. Most of the learners have spent so many years studying in conventional face to face interaction hence they need time and space to switch over to this new system. To make the transition from face to face interaction to self-learning system smoothly various student support services are available in distance learning.

Student Support Service

Student support service refers to a variety of non-academic interactions that the student has with an institution. These include pre-enrolment services, admissions, and registrations, academic advising, financial planning and management, library and bookstore services, academic and career counseling, social support services, degree and transcript auditing and technical support. These service centers also need to provide adequate access to an appropriate range of student support services including admissions, financial aids, advising, delivering of course materials and placement and counseling.

Objectives of Student Support Services

The main aim of student support service is to make the learner self-reliant. Studying at home with the help of self-instructional material without having proper assistance from a teacher the learner may face lots of academic and personal problems. To remove these difficulties the student support services are devised. The other objectives of student support services are to encourage and support the students to motivate when they are discouraged in learning; to give feedback and responses to their assignments to go further in their learning; to clarify their queries, confusions and doubts about the study material and to assist the learner in proper planning, help them develop sound study skills appropriate to distance learning. The study canters which are linked with main institution through regional canters provide counseling, workshops, personal contact programmes etc.

Need for Counselling in Distance Education

In any traditional or conventional education teacher interacts with the students face-to-face. The major activities of teaching providing feedback, passing on information, evaluation, and advising are able to perform in a regular education, whereas, in distance education informing, advising, clarifying could not be performed. Hence, students or learners under distance education need somebody to assist him/her. This assistance may be in the form of providing general information, giving advice on appropriate cause of action or helping the students to meet their needs, or solve their problems related to their study. A part from these, there is various types of barriers which may affect the learners' study process. These barriers may be study related; time-related; personal and institutional. To overcome these barriers the learner in distance education needs counselling.

Personal Contact Programme

There are both advantages and disadvantages in distance learners from the conventional learner. The distance learner study independently without having the opportunity to interact with their teachers and peer- group regularly. The learner is independent and has to do each and every thing to solve his problems on his own.

This situation may generate feeling of loneliness, helplessness, demonization and in turn affects the pace and ability of the learner. To avoid this problem the distance education organizes personal contact programme, or a place where the distance learner enjoy the facility of interacting with the teachers and the peer-group face to face. During the contact programme the learner can manipulate or utilize the opportunity to have in-depth knowledge of the subject matter.

Enhancing the Quality of Student Support Service

The above two programmes namely, counselling and personal contact programmes could be strengthened to enhance the distance learners.

a. Personal Contact Programme

The personal contact programme can be organized systematically. It should be made compulsory for the students to attend. Some incentives or recognitions could be given in the form of marks or grade. In the contact programme the learner must be given enough time and opportunity to interact with the teachers and the peer group. Regular classes could be arranged to discuss the various topics under the guidance of a supervisor. This method has been working effectively in the National Correspondence college of Zambia.

b. Study Centers

The study centers could be strengthened with regular orientation meetings, tutorials, visiting lecture, volunteer help groups etc. These centers must be equipped with enough rooms and library facilities. Only the centers having these facilities or able to give these facilities must be recognized as study centers. There must be periodic checking, evaluation and assessing to ensure the quality of the centers as well as the learners. The university Sains Malaysia, Penang follows this well knitted study centers. Each study centre under a particular institution must also be linked in service, facilities etc.

c. Use of Educational Technology

Educational technology could also be used to enhance the distance learners. The Indira Gandhi National Open University provides assistance to the students by making use of the available networks- internet, TV, Radio; Audio-video multimedia packages etc. by using the technology even a distance learner in a remote area could be benefitted.

d. Inclusive Student Services Process Model

Whatever we do in distance education system it should be student oriented. Their needs should be fulfilled. Hence, Miller and Princes (1976) proposed a model called Inclusive Student Service Process Model. There are five phases of student support services: learner intake, learner intervention, learner support, learner transition, and measurement of effectiveness.

1. *Learner intake phase*

Setting goals and assessing students' readiness for learning, including their desire ad ability to engage in distance learning are the key tasks during the learner intake phase. This phase also provides the learner the information on available financial resources as well as on procedures for applying for and receiving financial aid.

2. *Learner Intervention Phase*

The primary goal during this second phase is to assist students in self-development and independent learning. Support strategies offered in this phase include instruction on student success strategies, student help desk support, technology training, and online faculty advising.

3. *Learner Support Phase*

In this phase students learn self-development strategies so that they can accept responsibility for developing their own skills. Key support services during this phase are academic advising, instructional support and tutoring, library and bookstore services, disability services, and networking. They also must offer study tips, test-taking tips, and external instructional resources such as tutoring.

4. *Learner Transition Phase*

Career development and counselling services are key during this phase; helping students build their professional resumes, develop interviewing strategies, and deal with life issues are instrumental in retaining students.

5. *Measurement Phase*

This phase is important because it ensures that institutions focus on accountability and use feedback about student services programme in order to continually improve.

Taken together, these five phases of the Inclusive Student Services Process Model provide a systems approach to support students in meaningful ways, regardless of campus location or instructional delivery system.

Conclusion

Enrolment in distance education is rapidly increasing. Distance learners expect student support services to accommodate them from their point of entry through completion of their course. They expect rapid responses to requests for advising, career and academic counselling services, and library resources. Traditional services such as admissions, advising, registration, financial aid, career services, counselling, and library services must be reframed to incorporate strategies that meet the needs of technologically oriented student population. Hence, to implement student support services successfully in the twenty-first century the faculty and staff pragmatically and systematically redefine traditional student support services and implement the above five phase Inclusive Model to ensure success for all distance learners.

References

1. Deborah L. Floyd, Deborah Casey-Powell. New Roles for Student Support Services in Distance Learning. In New Directions for Community Colleges, 2004, 128.
2. Distance Education: Indira Gandhi National Open University School of Education, Delhi.
3. Sandhi, S. Student Support and Progression. In total Quality management in Teacher Education, St.Xavier's College of Education, Palayamkottai, 2008.

32

Factors Affecting Quality in Distance Education

Introduction

Education plays vital role in developing the personality of an individual as well as the economy of a nation. It has opened avenues for new industries, has enriched the functioning of the existing industries, has created lot of job opportunities, and has minimized the complexities of life and helps to lead happy and comfortable life. Though formal education serves as an elixir, it is not able to reach all the segments of society. Distance education satisfies the requirements of many learners who are deprived of formal education.

Need and Importance of Distance Education

The concept of distance learning has emerged in various countries of the world. The following points highlight the need and importance of distance education:

1. Explosion of knowledge: There is explosion of knowledge because of rapid scientific and technological developments. The formal system of education on account of its rigidity and high cost, finds it difficult to incorporate new changes speedily as desired.

2. *Population Explosion*: Unprecedented growth rate of population has resulted in the corresponding increase in students. The formal education system serves a selected and limited number of students.

3. *Varied Needs*: Distance learning is needed to satisfy the varied needs of varied students. It can be used to teach people of different ages and to teach courses from a wide range of discipline areas. It is especially needed for those who want to learn while learning.

4. *Desire to Improve Qualification & Self – Improvement*: There are many people who want to improve their education qualification while they are in jobs. Distance learning provides opportunities to such people to improve their qualifications. It is needed from the point of view of self-learning and self-improvement of an individual who, otherwise is deprived of receiving proper education.

5. *Geographical and Social Isolation*: People may be geographically isolated because a communication system has not been developed. They may be socially isolated or disadvantaged due to financial, physical, emotional or family circumstances. It provides opportunities to large number of people who had previously been denied such opportunities.

6. *Democratic Aspirations and Universal Education*: Distance learning is needed to meet the great demand for democratization of education from those sections of society that is neglected. It is needed to achieve the cherished goal of the nation for universalization of education.

Factors that affect the Quality of Distance Education

While distance education has been in existence for many years, the medium has changed from pencil & paper correspondence course to real-time Internet courses. But regardless of the medium, it has common characteristics and, likewise has similar problems.

Student – The distance students neither get feedback nor have contact with the teacher. They lack support services such as providing tutors, academic planners and schedulers and technical assistance. Many students are not well versed in the uses of Computers and Internet.

Faculty – Faculty experience problems such as lack of staff training in course development and ICT technology. As many distance education courses are different from traditional courses, it imposes a burden on teachers who already have been trained for traditional classrooms.

Organisation – Technology considerations are self-evident but are the most easily solved. Technology problems include; financing new technology, telecommunications, hardware issues, course production and technology, and Internet problems.

Course Considerations – Many believe, distance courses are inferior to traditional courses. Curriculum and assessment materials are not as good as traditional materials. Institution need to maintain the same course content, learning objectives, standards, and credits for all the sections, regardless of method of delivery.

Research Undertaken

A research had been done to find out the factors affecting the quality of distance education. A tool was developed and administered to teachers who were graduated by Distance education institution and Formal education institution as well. The following table describes the findings of the study.

S.No	Statements	Teachers' opinion about Distance Education		Teachers' opinion about Formal Education	
		Yes (%)	No(%)	Yes(%)	No(%)
1	Completion of syllabus within the stipulated time.	44.12	55.88	94.12	5.88
2	Giving adequate importance to explain the difficult concepts	38.24	61.76	94.12	5.88
3	Proving necessary assistance in the learning process.	52.94	47.06	82.35	17.65
4	Use of multimedia for better teaching.	11.79	88.24	38.24	61.76
5	Opportunity to interact with teacher to clear your doubts.	50.00	50.00	94.12	5.88
6	Providing well-structured students' hand book.	44.12	55.88	76.47	23.53
7	Provided necessary Course materials/Books on time.	76.47	23.53	88.24	11.76
8	Informing about reference books for different subjects.	38.24	61.76	91.18	8.82
9	Use of Course materials/Books provided by the institutions.	76.47	23.53	85.29	14.71
10	Appropriate guidance regarding question pattern & examination.	67.65	32.35	94.12	5.88
11	Inspiration to learn the subject more.	52.94	47.06	91.18	8.82
12	Proper evaluation of assignments.	38.24	61.76	91.18	8.82

13 Subject teachers - real experts in their field of study.	73.53	26.47	85.29	14.71
14 Resolving grievances within the time limit.	32.35	67.65	64.71	35.29
15 Informing about the activities of the course well in advance.	52.94	47.06	82.35	17.65
16 Publication of results within a reasonable time limit.	55.88	44.12	97.06	2.94
17 Use of latest technologies for effective learning and smooth conduct of the course.	14.71	85.29	38.24	61.76
18 Practical value of learnt material.	52.94	47.06	82.35	17.65
19 Providing necessary educational, vocational & personal guidance	52.94	47.06	82.35	17.65
20 Striking a balance between education and personal affair.	58.82	41.18	61.76	38.24

Findings

1. 88.24% teachers have said that multimedia was not used for better teaching.
2. 85.29% teachers have stated that latest technology was used neither for effective learning nor for the smooth conduct of the course.
3. 67.65% teachers have said that their grievances were not resolved within the time limit.
4. 61.76% teachers have said that adequate importance was not given, neither to explain difficult concepts nor to inform about reference books for different subjects. They have also expressed that their assignments were not evaluated properly.
5. 55.88% teachers have expressed that syllabus was not completed within the stipulated time and they were not provided with well-structured students' hand book.

Conclusions

1. Distance Education Institutions must take necessary steps to enrich teaching by explaining difficult concepts, using multimedia and completing syllabus within the stipulated time.
2. They should provide well-structured students' hand book and also details about reference books for different subjects and
3. They should take adequate measures to ensure accurate evaluation and to resolve students' grievances.

33

Technology Mediated Learning in Distance Education

Introduction

Distance Education is a broad term that refers to the process of delivering a specific curriculum to the learners who are not physically present on campus. Recent technological advances, along with changing learner demographics have triggered a significant rise in the popularity of this type of education. As distance education has evolved, it has become inextricably linked to technology.

Distance learning is one of the most rapidly growing innovations in higher education today. It has been instrumental in increasing student populations and in better serving the needs of existing students at many institutions. Faculties who prepare distance learning courses have the responsibility of delivering these courses with the same instructional rigor as on-campus courses.

The challenges posed by distance education are countered by opportunities to:

- Reach a wider student audience

- Meet the needs of students who are unable to attend on-campus classes
- Involve outside speakers who would otherwise be unavailable
- Link students from different social, cultural, economic, and experiential backgrounds

Electronic Networks:

In recent years, educators have witnessed the rapid development of computer networks. Dramatic improvements are seen in the processing power of personal computers and striking advances in storage technology. These developments have made the computer a dynamic force in distance education, providing a new and interactive means of overcoming time and distance to reach learners. Millions of pages of graphics and text-based information can be accessed directly online through hundreds of public, private and commercial networks, including the biggest network of all: the Internet.

Computers in Distance Education

Computer applications for distance education fall into four broad categories:

- **Computer Assisted Instruction (CAI)** - uses the computer as a self-contained teaching machine to present discrete lessons to achieve specific but limited educational objectives. There are several CAI modes, including: drill and practice, tutorial, simulations and games, and problem-solving.
- **Computer Managed Instruction (CMI)** - uses the computers branching, storage, and retrieval capabilities to organize instruction and track student records and progress. The instruction need not be delivered via computer, although often CAI (the instructional component) is combined with CMI.
- **Computer Mediated Communication (CMC)** - describes computer applications that facilitate communication.

Examples include electronic mail, computer conferencing, and electronic bulletin boards.

- **Computer-Based Multimedia**- HyperCard, hypermedia, and a still-developing generation of powerful, sophisticated, and flexible computing tools have gained the attention of distance educators in recent years. The goal of computer-based multimedia is to integrate various voice, video, and computer technologies into a single, easily accessible delivery system.

Advantages of Computers

1. Computers can facilitate self-paced learning. In the CAI mode, for example, computers individualize learning, by giving immediate reinforcement and feedback.
2. Computers are a multimedia tool. With integrated graphic, print, audio, and video capabilities, computers can effectively link various technologies. Interactive video can be incorporated into computer-based instructional units, lessons, and learning environments.
3. Computers are interactive. Microcomputer systems incorporating various software packages are extremely flexible and maximize learner control.
4. Computer technology is rapidly advancing. Innovations are constantly emerging, while related costs drop. By understanding their present needs and future technical requirements, the cost-conscious educator can effectively navigate the volatile computer hardware and software market.
5. Computers increase access. Local, regional, and national networks link resources and individuals, wherever they might be. In fact, many institutions now offer complete undergraduate and graduate programs relying almost exclusively on computer-based resources.

The Internet and Distance Education

The Internet is the largest, most powerful computer network in the world. It encompasses 1.3 million computers with Internet addresses that are used by up to 30 million people in more than fifty countries. As more and more colleges, universities, schools, companies, and private citizens connect to the Internet either through affiliations with regional not-for-profit networks or by subscribing to information services provided by for-profit companies, more possibilities are opened for distance educators to overcome time and distance to reach students.

With access to the Internet, distance educators and their students can use:

- **Electronic mail (e-mail) -** Like postal mail, e-mail is used to exchange messages or other information with people. Instead of being delivered by the postal service to a postal address, e-mail is delivered by Internet software through a computer network to a computer address.
- **World-Wide Web (WWW)** -The WWW is an exciting and innovative front-end to the Internet. Officially WWW is described as a "...wide-area hypermedia information retrieval initiative aiming to give universal access to a large universe of documents". The WWW provides Internet users with a uniform and convenient means of accessing the wide variety of resources (pICTures, text, data, sound, and video) available on the Internet.

Teaching Considerations

When incorporating the Internet into a distance delivered course, we need to remember that,

- All students in a course must have Internet and WWW access to ensure equal opportunities for computer interaction and feedback. Also, convenient access to a computer at home or work may influence student success.

- Students may face the concurrent challenges of learning basic computer skills, new software, and appropriate online communication skills. Setting up a specific classroom conference for ongoing discussions of specific hardware and software problems may help students to work through these problems on their own.
- Some students might hesitate to contribute to send e-mail because of a lack of familiarity with the proper protocols. Encourage students to use e-mail, electronic bulletin boards, and the WWW early in the course so they overcome inhibitions. Specifying a minimum number of e-mail communications per week will encourage active participation.
- Using e-mail can help the instructor provide feedback more quickly than surface mail or telephone. Prompt response generally increases student motivation and performance.

Virtual Reality-An Emerging Technology:

Virtual reality offers the promise of training future students in ways that currently are far too dangerous or expensive. Virtual reality combines the power of computer generated graphics with the computer's ability to monitor massive data inflows in real time to create an enclosed man/machine interactive feedback loop. VR participants wearing visors projecting the computer images react to what they see while sensors in the visor and body suit send information on position and the head and eye movement of the wearer. The computer changes the scene to follow the wearer and give the impression of actually moving within an artificial environment.

Personal Digital Assistants

Apple's introduction of personal digital assistants (PDAs) has opened a new realm of freedom and power for computing and telecommunications users that could well have important implications for educational users. PDAs provide a screen that can interpret what is written on it with a stylus and convert that to text. These handheld devices currently are used to send and receive fax messages via cellular telephone technology, store calendars, store telephone numbers and dial them for voice communications, and can send and receive data with the user's desktop computer.

Conclusion

These new technologies can lead to more empowerment and thus contribute more for learner control instruction for distance education students. Networks have the potential of providing a broad knowledge base to citizens around the world, and will offer opportunities for expanded applications of distance education also. However these Future emerging technologies will change the system of learning through Distance mode.

References:

1. Barnard, J. (1992). Multimedia and the future of distance learning technology. *Educational Media International, 29* (3), 139-144.

2. Bates, A. W. (1987). *Television, learning and distance education.* Milton Keynes, UK: The Open University, Institute of Educational Technology.

3. Brew, A., & Wright, T. (1990). Changing teaching styles. *Distance Education, 11* (2), 183-212.

4. Tania H. Gottschalk, Editor , "Distance Education at a Glance Home" Engineering Outreach, University of Idaho.

34

Attitude of Ignou B.Ed. Trainees Towards Distance Education

Introduction

Education is as old as the human race. Its importance has been realized since times immemorial and it continues right upon this day. It has been accepted as one of the primary needs of every civilized person. But education as a basic necessity for human beings is not made available to everyone cheap or in plenty. All those who need it may be monetarily well off. Further, the availability of institutions may be a hindrance because sufficient number of institutions is not made available though the number of applications for admission does not keep pace with the number of seats available in higher education institutions. In an attempt to solve such problems, distance education has been considered as an alternative which denoted the application of multi-media approach during the entire learning process.

Education is as old as the human race. Its importance has been realized since times immemorial and it continues right upon this day. It has been accepted as one of the primary needs of every civilized person. But education as a basic necessity for human beings is not made available to everyone cheap or in plenty. All those who need it may be monetarily well off. Further, the availability of institutions may be a hindrance because sufficient number of institutions is not made available though the number of applications for admission does not keep pace with the number of seats available in higher education institutions. In an attempt to solve such problems, distance education has been considered as an alternative which denoted the application of multi-media approach during the entire learning process.

The need for such education which could be provided to an individual at his own pace gave berth to the concept of distance education. Now a day, no one can deny the need of education to improve the life style and living standards. It has been realized all over the world that the prevailing formal system of education is not sufficient to meet the demands of the masses and bring equity in education. Constraints in terms of human resources and finances to build educational institutions, appointment of teachers and distance of the students from the schools or colleges etc. has resulted in an alternative system of education which could be used to expand education both quantitatively and qualitatively and fulfil educational needs of all. Instead of bringing students to the educational institutions, it has proposed to take school to the students and hence, the concept of education came into existence.

Distance Education is one of the most important educational innovations of the twentieth century. It is considered as the most important part of the overall educational system. During the last decade, because of the frequent changes in society, different educational systems have come into being. Particularly because of the wide expansion of educational technology, there came the realization of the inadequacy of conventional face-to-face system of education. Further, due to incompatibility of accommodating the growing needs of the society, effective alternative educational systems were born. 'Distance System' was one among them. An upsurge of enrolment rate in the educational institutions is one of the vital factors that makes distance mode of teaching and learning a social imperative. There is no doubt that distance education is an effective alternative to the formal education. The distance education programme aims at educating those who for one reason or the other are not able to join a college or university. There are a very large number of employed adults who want to acquire knowledge and earn a degree. Such persons, however, find themselves in a position of helplessness as they cannot afford any sort of disruption in their employment. The number of such persons too is unlimited who otherwise are very keen to go in for higher education, but they do not fit in with the normal admission criteria of our universities, with the result their aspirations remain unfulfilled. Here comes distance education to help such people and caters to the needs of such classes of society. Thus, it complements the formal educational system.

Distance education is an educational mode supplementary, complementary and alternative to conventional/traditional system of education, depending on the situation it was practiced. Today it has evolved into an independent system of education, thanks to the growth of communication technologies and the cognitive sciences which are flexible enough to use the technologies for pedagogic purposes. It is an educational innovation to meet the ever increasing and diversified educational needs and demands of the society which are sequel to changing social, economic and other conditions on one hand and technological developments on the other.

Distance Education defined

Wedemeyer (1977) has used the terms 'open learning', 'distance education' and 'independent study' in his works, but favours 'independent study' consistently. Independent study consists of various forms of teaching – learning arrangements in which teachers and learners carry out their essential tasks and responsibilities apart from one another, communicating in a variety of ways. Its purposes are to free on-campus or internal learners from inappropriate class placing or patterns, to provide off-campus or external learners with the opportunity to continue learning in their own environments, and developing in all learners the capacity to carry on self- directed learning, the ultimate maturity required of the educated person. Moore (1973)defined distance education as the family of instructional methods in which the teaching behaviours are performed apart from learning behaviours, including those that in a contiguous situation would be performed in the learner's presence, so that communication between the teacher and the learner must be facilitated by print, electronic, mechanical or other devices. Dohmen (1977) defined distance education as a systematically organized form of self-study in which student counselling, the presentation of learning material and securing and supervising of students' success is carried out by a team of teachers, each of whom has responsibilities. It is made possible at a distance by means of media which can cover long distances.

Peters (1973) defined distance education as a method of imparting knowledge, skills and attitudes which is rationalized by the application of division of labour and organizational principles as well as by the extensive use of technical media, especially for the purpose of reproducing high quality teaching material which makes it possible to instruct great numbers of students at the same time wherever they live. It is an industrialized form of teaching and learning. Holmberg (1981)defined distance education as that kind of education which covers the various forms of study at all levels which are not under continuous, immediate supervision of tutors present with their students in lecture rooms on the same premises, but which, nevertheless, benefit from the planning, guidance and tuition of a tutorial organization. Keegan (1990) brings together the various aspects of all the above definitions in order to clarify the nature of distance education. These aspects are follows.

1. The teacher and the learner are separated from each other and this is a central characteristic of this form of education.
2. Distance education is an institutional kind of educational system. It is, therefore, distinct from private study which may

result from private reading or watching TV or attending a talk, etc.

3. Distance education makes use of the various technically advanced media such as printing, telephone, audio-video, broadcasting, computer, etc.
4. It is a two way communication because the student is able to respond through assignment-responses or other media and therefore can receive feedback. The student thus enters into a dialogue with the institution.
5. Each student is separated from his / her peer group in the sense that although the learners form a fairly sizeable population, they do not have face-to-face interaction among themselves. Thus, distance education becomes a highly individualized learning system. In this sense, it remains one of the most individualized of all educational systems. Even though study groups may be formed under distance education learning programmes, these may not be compulsory and the student is free to work entirely on his / her own.
6. Distance education is a specific answer to a specific need. It is the industrial society that has created a need for a more capsular kind of education. At the same time, it is the same society that has developed the necessary technology to be able to structure an educational system that will cater to such a specialized kind of need for education.

In a nut shell, distance education may be defined as that field of educational endeavour in which 1. The learner is quasi-permanently separated from the teacher throughout the length of the learning process, 2.The learner is quasi-permanently separated from the learning group throughout the length of the learning process, 3.A technological medium replaces the interpersonal communication of conventional, oral group-based education, 4.The teaching / learning process is institutionalized and 5. Two way communications is possible between both the student and the teacher.

Distance education system started functioning with the following as objectives. (a) To provide facilities to pursue higher education to all qualified and willing persons who are unable to join regular college / university courses because of personal reasons like pre-occupation, social and family life commitments etc., and economic reasons like poverty etc., or because of their inability to obtain admission in a regular college / university, (b) To provide educational facilities to those persons who are having necessary desire to acquire further knowledge and improve their professional competence, (c) To provide opportunities and academic pursuits of educated citizens for improving their standard of knowledge and learning through distance education without get disturbed their present employment, (d) To help the socially and economically backward sections of the society to become educated, (e) To carry the school / college to the pupils or to take the fruits of useful learning to the very door step of pupils, (f) To provide educational opportunities for the personnel who are in need of distance education like in service persons who due to economic or other reasons take up jobs at a early age but are looking for an opportunity to improve their educational qualifications, drop outs who later become motivated to complete their education, persons residing in geographically remote rural areas where institutions of higher education are not made available, retired personnel who are interested to take up studies to keep themselves occupied, persons who studies just for the love of it, or to satisfy their curiosity, handicapped persons, persons requiring some additional training in their vocation for updating their knowledge and skills in teaching various subjects etc.

Distance education system, in comparison to conventional system, is more advantageous as it has its implications at various levels of teaching like primary, secondary and higher education, supplements the studies of regular students along with being a separate system of education, provides for learning in one's own speed, is very much flexible in terms of time and place and is conducive to greater variety of subjects of study, promotes self-learning and self-improvement, improves technical and vocational skills, provides education to any remote or far-off areas through non-print media like radio, television, etc., fulfil the needs of various categories of persons, promotes the development of man power resources in the country, entertains study in privacy, makes higher education accessible to all sections of society, doesn't required more full time staff members and buildings, is more economical and finally distance education system helps to achieve the cherished goal of the nation for universalization of education. Thus 'Distance Education' as a non-formal system touches all the three dimensions of learning like cognitive, affective and psychomotor.

Learners enrol to various courses / programmes offered under distance education system for many reasons. The successful completion of the course or the programme by the learners depends upon their intellectual and emotional satisfaction with the course / programme provided by the system. This will lead to have a positive and favourable attitude towards distance education system. Greater the satisfaction in completion of the course, more favourable the attitude will be towards distance education system.

Attitude Defined

Attitude is normally defined as a generalized pattern in perception or action towards an object or thing as in integration of various experiences. Travers (1973) defined attitude as a readiness to respond in such a way that behaviour is given a certain situation. This means that attitude is responsible for behaving in a particular and definite way. If one keeps a positive and favourable attitude towards an object, he will be attracted towards it; he will admire it and try to achieve it. On the other hand, if one has a negative or unfavourable attitude, one will try to avoid it and even feel hostile to it. Sorenson (1943) defined attitude as a particular feeling about something. It, therefore, involves a tendency to behave in a certain way in situations which involve that something, whether person, idea or object. It is partially rational and partially emotional and is acquired, not inherent, in an individual. This explains why an individual behaves in a certain way when he is needed to respond to a particular object for which he has developed a positive or negative attitude. He has some what a definite set of feelings, likes or dislikes for that object which partly stands on rational and partly on emotional footings. But they are all acquired and learned through varying experiences. Mckeachie and Doyle (1966) defined attitude as an organization of concepts, beliefs, habits and motives associated with a particular object. Further it is referred as what one thinks, feels and how he reacts does, expresses one's attitude towards an object. By critically examining the above, attitude can be understood as a determining acquired tendency which prepares a person to behave in a certain way towards a specific object or class of object subjects to the conditions prevailing in the environment.

Formation or development of attitudes depends upon certain factors which are found within the individual himself and individual's environment. Environmental forces help an individual to form or develop various attitudes. An attitude at any stage is essentially a product of the interaction of one's self with one's environment. In educational context, the atmosphere of the school and classroom, the behaviour of teachers, schoolmates, and classmates, the methods of teaching, curriculum, discipline and procedure for evaluation etc., affects the formation of attitude towards the educational system.

Similarly even in distance education system, the attitude of distance learners towards the instructional system will be affected by the various factors of learning environment like procedure for admission, mode of instruction including the presentation of content through multimedia viz, print media like self-instructional material and non-print media like, telecasting radio and television programmes related to various course content, assignments – their method of evaluation and feedback, personal contact programmes in terms of counselling sessions and workshops, functioning of study centers in meeting the intellectual and emotional needs of the distance learners, mode of evaluation in terms of continuous assessment and term end examination etc.

Need and Importance

The concept of distance education is gaining importance in the various advanced, underdeveloped and developing especially to meet the new aspirations of the people emerging because of explosion of knowledge, population and needs. Due to the explosion of knowledge in science and technology, the formal system of education due to its rigidity and higher cost, find it difficult to incorporate new changes speedily as desired. Consequently, the knowledge acquired in schools and colleges would soon become out-dated. It can be updated by some means of distance education. Due to population explosion, there has occurred a large increase in number of students. The formal education is not able to provide education to all those students due to one or the other reasons like limited number of seats in schools and colleges especially professional courses, admission and examination requirements, full time and long study periods, courses which are not related to the socio-economic requirements of the society, formalism and pressure of examinations, high cost of education, etc. It is used to educate people of different ages and to educate courses from a wide range of discipline areas, both vocational and non-vocational. Distance education contributes a lot to attain the cherished goal of nation for universalization of education. It is essential to meet the great demand for democratization of education from those sections of society especially neglected. It is able to provide opportunities to a large number of people who had previously been denied such opportunities. It fulfils the educational need of people who are geographically isolated due to distance or lack of communication system. Distance education is useful for such people who are socially isolated or disadvantaged because of financial, physical, emotional or family circumstances. It is essential for the point of need of self-learning and self-improvement of an individual who, otherwise, has been deprived of receiving proper education. Since the varied interest of the students could not be satisfied by formal system of education, distance education is essential for satisfying the varied needs of varied students. Distance education is especially helpful and useful to those who want to learn while earning.

There are many people who have a great desire to improve their qualifications while they are on jobs. Distance education provides opportunities to such people for improving their qualifications.

Distance education provides second chance to enable people to improve their qualifications, carrier prospects and skills while they are in service. High rate of enrolment, alternate mode for improvement of academic status and skills with bare minimum inputs have contributed to the evolution of distance education. The need is to introspect the development of the system and be prepared for the future challenges of the system.

Distance education, thus, has now earned the credibility of a viable and an effective alternative channel for imparting education at all levels all over the world and India is no exception to it. This system is gaining popularity day by day. It should strive to achieve international standards through professional practices.

Distance education system is gaining popularity day by day and here the need for research in distance education. There is a steady increase in the number of studies in the area of distance education. Various aspects of this innovation system have attracted the attention of the educational researchers. They have mainly looked into its relevance, need motivating factors, characteristics, growth and development, study centers, personal contact programmes, development and production of course materials, submission of assignments, industrial process, evaluative measures etc.

Review of related literature reveals that studies have been conducted to know the learners, teachers and society's attitude towards the various aspects of this innovative mode of education. But in the Indian context, very few researchers (Khan, 1982; Ram, 1984; Sahoo and Bhat, 1987; Panda and Chaudhari, 1989; Renu, 1990; Pandey, 1991; Nagpal, 1992) have made attempts to measure distance learner's attitude towards distance education which forms only a part of their studies. Review of literature also reveals that rarely attempt has been made to find out the attitude of distance learners of professional courses, especially of B.Ed. course with respect to various biographical variables like sex, age, educational qualifications, type of working institution, levels of teaching, regional background, marital status, subjects specialization, etc. as the formation or development of attitude will vary with respect to the above variables. From the review it also becomes clear that number of studies which measures the attitude of teacher trainees towards various dimensions of distance education were rarely reported. This calls for the need to take up a study to find out the attitude of B.Ed. trainees towards distance education with respect to various biographical variables. Hence, the problem is stated as follows.

A thorough review of related literature revealed that the studies have mainly looked into its relevance, need motivating factors, characteristics, growth and development, study centers, personal contact programmes, development and production of course materials, submission of assignments, instructional process, evaluative measures, etc. Review of related literature also revealed that studies have been conducted by researchers (Sorenson (1948), Prahalad, (1978), Indradevi (1985), SahooandBhat (1987), Mani, Gomathi (1989), Srinivasacharyulu, Rao and Mouli (1989), Panda and Chaudhari (1989), Arun, Renu (1990), Ashalatha (1990), Mandal, Sushmita and Shah, Anupama (1992), Srinivasacharyulu and Ramaiah (1992), Rajendraprasad and John (1992), *Sengupta (1993), Reddy (1994), Sahoo (1994), Sinha, Arvind et.al. (1994), Devi (1994), Shin and Maxwell (2003), Lakshmiprasanna (2005), to find out the attitude of distance learners towards distance education and obtained mixed results.*

Attitude of participants and the community towards distance education has been treated as one of the criteria in studying the success of distance education. A survey of employed persons in Kerala, mainly clerks with bachelor's degrees revealed that evening college education was preferred to correspondence courses for further education. However, the learners continuing with the distance education courses had expressed positive attitudes towards the system. In comparison with the male students, the female students had expressed more favourable attitude towards it and in the same way, employed students were more positive opinion towards distance education, whereas the remaining half were either neutral or negative about it. School (1985) revealed that even though distance teachers had positive attitude towards the system, around 71 per cent of them reported that they intended to leave the present positions and join regular college/departments, provided they get opportunities to do so. They expressed their views anticipating greater scope for research and professional growth in a conventional institution. Lakshmiprasanna (2005) conducted a study on attitude of KSOU M.Ed. Students towards distance education. The findings of the study were 1. 1. There was no significant difference between 1.male and female, 2.younger and older, 3.government and private aided 4.government and private unaided, 5.private aided and private unaided schools, 6.less and more teaching experience, 7.rural and urban background and 8.married and unmarried M.Ed. students of KSOU towards distance education. In short, what research says about distance education can be summarized as follows.

Despite their negative points, research on distance education has revealed quite a number of its positive aspects. They are:

1. Distance education is a blessing for common man
2. Distance education programme has proved its efficiency as a suitable mode of lifelong education
3. Distance Education is the best alternative to the formal system of education
4. Distance education has been perceived as a means of educational system for providing higher learning facilities to a large number of learners who could not pursue higher studies through regular courses
5. Distance education courses have gained popularity among employed group of learners though most of them could not sustain motivation to continue with studies till completion of the course

6. The didactic comments of the tutors/teachers on assignments provide a meaningful feedback to the learners
7. Students attending PCPs have positive opinion about the usefulness of the PCPs in terms of clarification of doubts, getting inspiration for further studies, better preparation for examination, solving academic problems and effective teacher-student interaction.

Review of the related literature reveals that the studies have been conducted to know the learners, teachers and society's attitude towards the various aspects of this innovative mode of education. But in the Indian context, very few researchers (Khan, 1982; Ram, 1984; Sahoo and Bhat, 1987; Panda and Chaudhari, 1989; Renu, 1990; Pandey, 1991; Nagpal, 1992) have made attempts to measure distance learner's attitude towards distance education which forms only a part of their studies. Review of literature also reveals that rarely attempt has been made to find out the attitude of distance learners of professional courses, especially of B.Ed. course with respect to various biographical variables like sex, age, educational qualifications, type of school in which they are working, levels of teaching, regional background, marital status, subjects of specialization, etc. towards distance education.

Teaching profession is the noble profession. The teachers are the builders of the nation. There is an urgent need to know about their attitude towards this profession, so that proper measures can be taken up to develop a positive attitude towards teaching profession. This has to be done at pre service teachers training it. Hence the advantages of distance education and the dearth of research in this field calls for the need to take up the present study. In the present study an attempt has been made to find out the significance of difference in the attitude of IGNOU B.Ed. students towards distance education.

Objectives of the Study

The objectives of the study were to find out the significance of difference between the attitudes of 1. Male and female, younger and older, less and more teaching experienced, rural and urban, married and unmarried B.Ed. trainees and 2.B.Ed. trainees working in government and private aided government and private unaided, private aided and private unaided schools towards distance education.

Hypothesis of the Study

The hypotheses were 1. There is no significant difference between the attitudes of 1. male and female, younger and older, less and more teaching experienced, rural and urban, married and unmarried B.Ed. trainees, and B.Ed. trainees working in government and private aided, government and private unaided, private aided and private unaided schools towards distance education.

Sample

The subjects of the study were 143 teacher trainees of IGNOU B.Ed. programme.of MES Teachers College Study Centre, Bangalore.

Tool

The data was collected by administering a tool entitled Kumar's Scale for Measuring Distance Learner's Attitude towards Distance Education.

Statistical Technique

T-test was used to test the significance of difference between the attitudes of B.Ed. trainees towards distance education with respect to the variable selected for the study.

Analysis and Interpretation of Data

Analysis of the Scores of Attitude of B.Ed. Trainees with respect to Sex, Age, Teaching Experience, Regional Background, Marital Status and Type of School for Various Dimensions of Distance Education

Comparison of the scores of attitude of male and female, younger and older, less and more teaching experienced, rural and urban, married and unmarried B.Ed. trainees, and B.Ed. trainees working in government and private aided, government and private unaided, private aided and private unaided schools towards distance education.

Major Hypothesis I

The differences in sex, age, teaching experience, regional background and marital status do not account for the significant differences in the attitude of B.Ed. trainees towards distance education

Hypothesis 1 to 5

There is no significant difference between the attitudes of 1. Male and female, 2.Younger and older, 3.less and more teaching experienced, 4. Rural and urban, 5.Married and unmarried B.Ed. trainees towards Distance Education.

Mean, Standard deviation, and t-value are computed for the scores of attitude of 1. Male and female, 2. Younger and older, 3. Less and more teaching experienced 4. Rural and urban, 5. Married and unmarried B.Ed. trainees towards distance education, and is presented in table – 1.

Table-1 : N, Mean, Standard deviation, and t-value of the Scores of Attitude of Male and Female, Younger and Older, Less and More Teaching Experienced, Rural and Urban, Married and Unmarried B.Ed. Trainees towards Distance Education

Sr. No.	Variable	N	Mean	SD	t – Value	Significance Level at 0.05/0.01
1	Male	35	228.48	21.35	1.645	Non-Significant
2	Female	108	235.15	19.99		

3. Younger	53	231.18	19.81	1.042	Non-Significant
4 Older	90	234.78	20.18		
5. Less Teaching Experienced	59	235.27	18.78	0.883	Non-Significant
6 More Teaching Experienced	84	232.33	20.66		
7. Rural	49	227.18	17.38	3.034	**Significant
8. Urban	94	237.07	20.47		
9. Married	106	232.30	28.39	0.310	Non-Significant
10.Unmarried	37	231.00	19.28		

**Significant at 0.01 level of Significance

As it is indicated in the table –1, the obtained t-value s are 1.645, 1.042, 0.883, and 0.310 are less than the table t-value 1.98, i.e., for 141 degrees of freedom at 0.05 level of significance. This means that there is no significant difference between the attitude of male and female, younger and older, less teaching experienced and more teaching experienced, and married and unmarried B.Ed. trainees towards distance education. Hence the null hypothesis 1, 2, 3, and 5 are accepted. From the table it can also be seen that the obtained t-value 3.034 is more than the table t-value 2.62 i.e., for 141 degrees of freedom at 0.01 level of significance. This indicates that there is a significant difference between the attitudes of B.Ed. trainees towards distance education. Hence the null hypothesis 4 is rejected and an alternative hypothesis is formulated stating that there is a significant difference between the attitudes of B.Ed. trainees towards distance education. The table also revealed that B.Ed. trainees (M=237.07) of urban background had better attitude towards distance education than the B.Ed. trainees (M= 227.18) of rural background.

Major Hypothesis II

The differences in type of school in which the B.Ed. trainees are working do not account for the significant differences in their attitude towards distance education

Hypothesis 6-8

There is no significant difference between the attitude of B.Ed. trainees working in government and private aided government and private unaided, and private aided and private unaided schools towards Distance Education.

Mean, Standard deviation, and t-value are computed for the scores of attitude of B.Ed. trainees working in government and private aided, government and private unaided, and private aided and private unaided schools towards distance education, and is presented in table-2.

Table-2 : N, Mean, Standard deviation, and t-value of the Scores of Attitude of B.Ed. Trainees working in Government and Private Aided, Government and Private Unaided, and Private Aided and Private Unaided Schools towards Distance Education

Sr. No.	Variable	N	Mean	SD	t – Value	Significance Level at 0.05/0.01
1	Government School	32	227.37	21.70	0.939	Non-Significant
2	Private Aided School	19	233.36	22.25		
3.	Government School	32	227.37	21.70	1.918	Non-Significant
4	Private Unaided School	92	235.60	18.46		
5.	Private Aided School	19	233.36	22.25	0.411	Non-Significant
6	Private Unaided School	92	235.60	18.46		

As it is indicated in the table – 2, the obtained t-values are 0.939, 1.918 and 0.411 are less than the table t- value 2.02, 1.98, 2.04, i.e., for 49, 122 and 29 degrees of freedom at 0.05 level of significance. This means that there is no significant difference between the attitude of B.Ed. trainees working in government and private aided government and private unaided and private aided and private unaided school towards distance education. Hence the null hypothesis 6, 7, and 8 are accepted.

Findings of the Study

The findings of the study were 1. There was no significant difference between the attitude of male and female, younger and older, less and more teaching experienced and married and unmarried B.Ed. trainees, and B.Ed. Trainees working in government and private aided, government and private unaided, private aided and private unaided schools. However a significant difference was found between the attitude of rural and urban background B.Ed. trainees towards distance education.

Conclusion

Based on the above findings it can be concluded that 1.sex, age, experience, marital status and the type of school in which B.Ed. trainees are working had no impact on their attitude towards distance education and 2. Differences in regional back ground had its impact on the attitude of B.Ed. trainees towards distance education. The attitude of urban B.Ed. trainees was found better than that of rural B.Ed. trainees towards distance education.

Educational Implications

Based on the results obtained with respect to the attitude of B.Ed. trainees of rural and urban background, it is implied that attitudinal change can be improved by extending the best possible services, to the rural trainees so as to enable them to make use of the benefits for their academic progress.

References

1. Arun, Renu. (1990). A Study of Success in Distance Learning System in Relation to Some Key Learner and Institutional Variables, Doctoral *Dissertation.* Kurukshetra University, Krurukshetra.
2. Ashalatha, J. (1990). Perceptions of Learners about Distance Education, M.Phil. Dissertation, Osmania University, Hyderabad.
3. Devi, U.M.D. (1994). Is Contact Session Necessary in Distance Education? *Indian Journal of Open Learning,* 3(1), 16-21.
4. Dohmen, G. (1977). *Das Fernstudium, Einneues Padagogisches Forschungs – Und Arbeitsfeld.* Tubingen: DIFF.
5. Holmberg, B. (1981). *Status and Trends of Distance Education.* London : Kogan Page.
6. Indradevi, V. (1985). *Philosophical Analysis of the Concept of Distance Education and its Implications on the Emerging Non-Formal System of Education with special reference to Teacher Education,* Doctoral Dissertation, Osmania University, Hyderabad.
7. Kaur, Ambika, S. (1995) Customer Expectation Satisfaction-A Case Study of Distance Education In Management, *Doctoral Dissertation*, Punjabi University, Patiala.
8. Keegan, D. (1990). Problem in Defining the Field of Distance Education. *The American Journal of Distance Education,* 17 (2), 4-11.
9. Khan, I. (1982). *Suitability of Teaching English through Correspondence Courses as Offered by Some Indian Universities at the First Degree Level.* Doctoral Dissertation. Bhubaneswar: Utkal University.
10. Kumar, A. (1999). *Kumar's Scale for Measuring Distance Learner's Attitude Towards Distance Education*, University News, 37 (2), 10-16.

11. Lakshmiprasanna (2005). A study of Attitude of KSOU M.Ed. Students. Unpublished M.Phil. Thesis. Karnataka State Open University, Mysore.

12. Mandal, Sushmita and Shah, Anupama (1992). Use of Modern and Conventional Media for Distance Education-An Experiment, Kakatiya Journal of Distance Education, 1(2), 46-57.

13. Mani, Gomathi (1989). *Attitude towards External Faculty towards Distance Education*, Paper Presented at ICDE Conference.

14. Moore, M.G. (1973). *Toward a Theory of Independent Learning and Teaching, Journal of Higher Education, 44*, 661 - 679

15. Nagpal, S. (1992). *Investigation Into the Usefulness of Distance Education.* Project Report, Diploma in Distance Education, New Delhi : IGNOU.

16. Panda, S.K. and Chaudhari, S.S. (1989). Attitude, Needs and Problems of Prospective Distance Teachers. *Media and Technology of Human Resource Development,2(1):*45- 53.

17. Pandey, S. (1991). *Teachers' Attitude towards Distance Education. Journal of Indian Education, 16* (5).

18. Peters,O. (1973). *Die didaktische ' Strukture des Fernunterrichts. Unterschungenzueinerindustrialisierten Form des Lehrens and Lernens,*Weinheim :Beltz.

19. Prahalad, S.R. (1978). *Application of Programmed Instruction to Distance Education,* M.Litt. Dissertation, Central Institute of English and Foreign Languages, Hyderabad.

20. Rajendraprasad, D. and John, E.A. (1992). *Development of Skills through teaching Practice- A Comparative Study of the Attitudes of B.Ed. trainees of distance and conventional Institutions, Kakatiya Journal of Distance Education,* 1(2), 90-91.c

21. Ram, S. (1984). *An Evaluation of Correspondence Education in Terms of Cost and Academic Performance.* Doctoral Dissertation, Meerut : Meerut University.

22. Reddy, V.R. (1994). *Learners Attitudes and Suggestions in Distance Education, in Distance Education: An Interface,* Hyderabad: BRAOU

23. Renu, A. (1990). *A study of Success in Distance Learning System in Relation to Some Key Learned and Institutional Variables.* Doctoral Dissertation, Kurukshetra :Kurukshetra University.

24. Sahoo, P.K. (1985). *A Study of the Correspondence Education in an Indian University.* Doctoral Dissertation. Baroda : M.S. University of Baroda.

25. Sahoo, P.K. (1994). Teleconferencing in Distance Education: IGNOU Experiment, *Indian Journal of Open Learning,* 3(1), 29-32.

26. Sahoo, P.K. and Bhat, V.D. (1987). Students Attitude Towards Correspondence System of Education. *Journal of Indian Education,* 13 (2), 28-33.

27. Sengupta, S. (1993).*Participant's Attitude towards Non-academic Staff Development at IGNOU, Media and Technology for Human Resource Development,* 5(4), 343-348

28. Shin amdMaxwell(2003). Factors related to Student Satisfaction and Motivation in Distance Science Learning: A Case Study of a Foundation Course in Biology and Earth Science. *Indian Journal of Open Learning,* 12(1,2). '7-27.

29. Sinha, Arvind et.al. (1994). *Interactive Communication for Distance Education: An Evaluative Study of ISRO-IGNOU Experiment,* ISRO Ahmadabad and IGNOU, New Delhi.

30. Sorenson, H. (1948). *Psychology in Education,* McGraw Hill Company, New York.

31. Srinivasacharyulu, G. and Ramaiah, P. (1992). *Face to Face Support Services at B.R. Ambedkar Open University: Student Response, Media and Technology for Human Resource Development,* 5(1), 41-47.

32. Srinivasacharyulu, G., Rao, S.C., and Mouli, R. (1989). *A Preliminary Study of Courses and Programmes, Center for Evaluation,* Andhra Pradesh University, Hyderabad.

33. Wedemeyer, C.A. (1977). Independent Study, A.S. Knowles (ed.). *The International Encyclopedia of Higher Education, 5, 2114-2132.*

35

Development and Validation of Self-instructional E-content Material on Tamil Teaching Methodology At B. Ed Level

Introduction

The imperative character of education for every one man now accepts individual growth and social development is a highly enterprising being. He is always on the lookout for inventing new innovations in all walks of like. Human like has improved tremendously as a result of the growth in science and technology. Education is a social institution that has also been influenced by technological development. The impact of changes is described as modernization. The teacher must concentrate on the media, which must initiate the learners to involve themselves in learning more the investigator being the Tamil graduate is interested to know the effectiveness of e-content in improving the delivery of inputs to our young generations.

Need For the Study

The information of the twenty first century which has been brought about by advance in the computer technology has created an information society in which majority of labor force are expected to hold information related jobs. In these days the unpredicted growth of interactive multimedia and e-content play a prominent in teaching Tamil in the field of education. In modern era the e-content plays a vital role in teaching. Now e-content by the teachers to enhance education is not unique. So investigator decided to do a study related to this area. Hence the researcher has chosen the development of e-content material in Tamil Teaching Methodology on B.Ed Trainees.

Objectives of the Study

i. To develop and design the e-content material in Tamil Teaching Methodology
ii. To develop e-content material in Tamil Teaching Methodology at B.Ed level.
iii. To validate the e-content material in Tamil based on the achievement test conducted to B.Ed Trainees.

Definition of the Key Term

e-content

"**e-content** is a package of data in an electronic digital form"

The term "e-content learning material" means the concept of packaging the knowledge (lessons) in the forms of presentations like PowerPoint, E-books, PDF format using Acrobat Reader and HTML file for educational instruction.

Development

Development refers to the production of the e-content which will undergo the various stages like pre-production, production, and post-production.

Validation

The assessment of the e-content in terms of certain identified parameters and establishment of its worthiness based on the achievement test.

Methodology Brief

The investigator followed the Experimental method for the present study. The data thus collected were put into appropriate statistical analysis. Mean, standard deviation, t-test.

Sampling Procedure

The main objective of this experimental research is to find out whether there exists a significant difference between the conventional method of teaching and the e-content method of teaching in Tamil teaching methodology through Electronic content to the B.Ed trainees in Oxford College of Education Trichy. The present study is concerned only to the 25 students from Tamil optional I students. By random sampling procedure, the researcher selected the College at random. Thus the sample college for present study is Oxford College of education trichy.

Data Analysis

't' test was applied to find out the significant difference, if any between the mean scores of the achievement of the groups under study.

Table – 4.1 : Analysis of pre-test and post-test scores between the Conventional methods and e-content method.

Group	N	mean	S.D	't' - value	Level of significance
Conventional method(pre-test)	25	8.2	1.356	3.703	0.05 level significant
e-Content method (post-test)	25	13.44	1.098		

The calculated value of 't' is 3.703, which is more than the critical value 2.02 at 0.005 level of significance. It implies that there is differences between the means scores under study are significant at 0.05 level of significance. Therefore the null hypothesis is rejected.

When we scrutinize the table it reveals that the performance of e-Content method is better than that of the conventional method in achievement. It is therefore concluded that the interactive Electronic Content has effectiveness on teaching Tamil Grammar in IX standard level compared to conventional teaching method.

Table – 4.2 : Analysis of Post-test scores between rural and urban students

Group	N	mean	S.D	't' - value	Level of significance
Rural	15	13.9	1.523		Not significant
Urban	10	12.7	1.417		

The calculated value of 't' is 0.82. it is less than the critical value 2.10 at 0.05 level of significance. It implies that the differences between the means scores under study. It is not significant at 0.01 and 0.05 level of significance. It is referred that the performances of the rural and urban students do not differ in the means scores significantly at Post-test level therefore the null hypothesis is accepted.

Findings of the Study

The following are the findings of the present study.

1. There is significant mean difference between the achievement of pre-test and post-test.
2. There is no significant mean difference between the achievement of rural and urban students in post-test.

Hypothesis - 1

There is no significant mean difference between the achievement of traditional teaching method and e-content teaching method.

Group Compared : Pre-test and Post-test

Data analyzed : Achievement scores

Statistical technique used : 't' test

Result :

Critical Value : 2.02 at 0.05 level

2.71 at 0.01 level

Interpretation : Null hypothesis is rejected because there is significant difference in the achievement scores of the pre-test and post-test. Thus it proves that there is a significant difference in the achievement scores in the subject in the pre-test and post-test there by providing that e-content package have significantly contributed to improve level achievement among the subjects of post-test(e-content teaching) group.

Hypothesis- 2

There is no significant mean difference in the mean scores of rural and urban students in the post-test..

Group Compared : Rural and urban students

Data analyzed : Achievement scores

Statistical technique used : 't' test

Result :

Critical Value : 2.02 at 0.05 level 2.71 at 0.01 level

Interpretation : Null hypothesis is accepted, because there is significant difference in the achievement scores of rural and urban students in the post-test group. Thus with regards of achievement it is proved that difference do not exist between rural and urban students there by indicating that level of achievement.

Educational Implication of the Study

The results of the study have proved that e-content is more effective than the traditional method in Tamil teaching methodology of B.Ed trainees when it is very effective then, it has to be equally effective to other standards also.

1. The use of the e-content enhances the achievement; it will diminish wastage and stagnation in school. So, a necessary orientation may be given at DIET level in order to create awareness among school teachers.

2. Video cassettes and audio cassettes can be developed based on the subject units by the NCERT, SCERT and even by the commercial agencies.

3. Keeping the result of study in mind the NCERT and SCERT should take up the work of providing modules as they produce teachers Hand Book and different e-content packages can be developed and supplied to all schools.

Conclusion

1. Technology has greatly improved the methods and educational opportunities available in the classroom. While there are some limitations which hold web based lessons back, the future certainly looks promising, and the continued development of web based lessons in surely to a new experience for many

students.

2. As far as Tamil is concerned, we have to gradually change our patterns of reasoning and advance to another level of understanding. This is a life-long process of change. It occurs when what we think we know about nature is not substantiated by our experiences, that someone nature does not quite make sense. "Knowing" is rooted in our innate desire to want understand ourselves and our environment. Hence, the primary task of hypermedia knows Tamil is to facilate these on-going changes in our mental processes as related to Tamil concepts. Thus, the e-content task is to provide a credible reality and a challenge to our existing mental processes, in short, to provide us into an appropriate level of cognitive conflict and motivated us to continue the process of knowing.
3. e-content provides us with some wonderful new approaches to this aspect of intrinsically motivating learning. E-content enables the Tamil teachers to provide our students with experiences of variable difficulty and randomness, simulating nature.

References

1. Good(CV) (1959) Foundations in Education. New York: McGraw Hill publishing Ltd.
2. Fredpercival And Elligton, Hury(1986) A hand book of educational technology, London: Kogan Page.
3. LEWIS, R and TAGG,E.D(eds)(1987) Trends in Computer Assisted Education. London: Black Well Scientific Publication.
4. Harrychand(1990) Techniques of teaching, New Delhi: A shish Publication House.
5. AchuthanSarala, et al,(1993). Computer Technology for Higher Education. Delhi: Concept Publishing Company.

6. Anderson,R.D., & MITCHENER C.P(1994). Research on science teacher Education, Hand book of research on science teaching and learning, New York Macmillan.

7. Goyal (Dr) (1998) Teacher preparation for computer Education, New Delhi: Sona Printer.

36

ICT Competency and Performance Competency of Distance Mode Students

Introduction

For longer than a decade, one of the key challenges to the professional development of teachers has been to help the integration of ICT into education. Rationales for an increase in ICT use are based on the assumption that the future will be dominated by knowledge-intensive professions, and employees need, therefore, sophisticated information processing skills and versatile ICT tools. Therefore, ICT in teaching is considered important in the facilitation of equal opportunities for citizens to study and develop their own knowledge to ensure the success and welfare of the nation. However, the implementation of ICT innovations into school practice is difficult. Thus, it is important to initiate research and development in this field in order to discover what contributes to successful adoption of these innovations.

Research literature has shown promising results on benefits of ICT use in education: it supports student collaboration and knowledge building. Further, in the context of teacher education, it offers possibilities for interaction with the nature; tools for real-time data logging. However, several problem issues have been identified which explain why ICT is not used in teaching in such extent as it could be appropriate according the potentials reported in the literature. Teachers feel a lack of up-to-date computer equipment and software. One interpretation could be that computers tend to be located in computer labs, not in ordinary classrooms or labs. The second interpretation could be that teachers have had insufficient time to learn about the use of ICT and its applications in classrooms consequently, they have no confidence in ICT use. Research suggests that in any topic, including the benefits of ICT in education, it has been difficult to change teachers' beliefs about teaching and learning. Teachers' beliefs have remained stable, and their resistance to change is one of the main explanations behind the diminutive adoption of ICT in education found evidence that teachers' beliefs regarding the usefulness of ICT in education appear to be surprisingly consistent across nations and cultures.

Computer technology has become a fundamental part of education in India and will likely be more so in the future. Unfortunately, Information Technology innovation initiatives in Tamilnadu are still characterized by a lack of research into possible options for policies and strategies. A key concern of this study was to assess the ICT competency and performance competency of distance mode B.Ed. students.

Objectives of the Study

1. To find out the level of ICT competency of distance mode B.Ed. students with reference to certain background variables.

2. To find out the level of performance competency of distance mode B.Ed. students with reference to certain background variables.

3. To find out the significant difference in ICT competency of distance mode B.Ed. students with reference to certain background variables.

4. To find out the significant difference in performance competency of distance mode B.Ed. students with reference to certain background variables.

5. To find out the significant correlation between performance competency and ICT competency of distance mode B.Ed. students with reference to certain background variables.

Hypotheses of the Study

1. The ICT competency level of distance mode B.Ed. students with reference to certain background variable is average.

2. The performance competency level of distance mode B.Ed. students with reference to certain background variable is average.

3. There is no significant difference in ICT competency of distance mode B.Ed. students with reference to certain background variables.

4. There is no significant difference in performance competency of distance mode B.Ed. students with reference to certain background variables.

5. There is no significant correlation between performance competency and ICT competency of distance mode B.Ed. students with reference to certain background variables.

Methodology

Sample

A total sample of 200 teachers was taken up for the present study. It consists of teachers who are studying B.Ed. degree in distance mode of Directorate of Distance Education, Madurai Kamaraj University, Madurai. Stratified random sampling technique is used for the selection of sample. The stratification has been done on the basis of gender, marital status and locality of the school.

Tools

The investigators developed and validated the tools to measure ICT Competency and Performance Competency.

1. **ICT competency scale:** This scale consists of 5 dimensions namely basic computer operation skill, word processing, spreadsheet, power point presentation and internet knowledge. The items have five responses namely not aware, little experience, occasional usage, regular user, confident and can explain. After the pilot study, 6 items had to be deleted from the draft and 40 items were selected for the final tool.

2. **Performance competency scale:** This scale consists of six major dimensions namely preparation, presentation, teacher behaviour, generalization, student-teacher interaction and classroom management with a 5 point rating scale as Unsatisfactory, Satisfactory, Good, Very Good, Excellent. The scoring was done by adding the ratings on the Teaching Competency Scale against all the items given by the investigator after observation of the teaching process by the teacher educators.

Data Collection

For the data collection, the investigators visited Nagercoil and Madurai B.Ed. study centre of DDE, Madurai Kamaraj University and collected the data from the respondents. The data were collected with the help of the developed tools. The questionnaire was distributed to the students and the investigators assured that their responses would be kept confidential and used for research purpose only. Clear instruction was given to enable them to give their response meaningfully. The gathered responses were scored.

Statistical Analysis

The data collected were analyzed by using descriptive and inferential analysis. The statistical techniques Percentage Analysis, 't' Test, and Pearson's Product-Moment Correlation were employed for the analysis and interpretation of the data.

Analysis of the Data

Table - 1 : The ICT competency level of distance mode B.Ed. students with reference to certain background variables

Background Variables	Category	Low		Average		High	
		No.	%	**No.**	%	**No.**	%
Gender	Male	11	23.9	26	56.5	9	19.6
	Female	30	19.5	101	65.6	23	14.9
Marital Status	Married	30	20.5	92	63.0	24	16.4
	Unmarried	10	18.5	36	66.7	8	14.8
Locality of School	Rural	20	21.1	60	63.2	15	15.8
	Urban	20	19.0	70	66.7	15	14.3

As far as ICT competency is concerned the average level of distance mode B.Ed. students is more than 50 percentage. So we can say that most of distance mode B.Ed. students are having average level of ICT competency. This may be due to the fact that the teachers are being provided with in-service trainings on educational technology and its innovations.

Table - 2 : The Performance competency level of distance mode B.Ed. students with reference to certain background variables.

Background Variables	Category	Low		Average		High	
		No.	%	**No.**	%	**No.**	%
Gender	Male	7	15.2	30	65.2	9	19.6
	Female	24	15.6	106	68.8	24	15.6

Marital Status	Married	23	15.8	101	69.2	22	15.1
	Unmarried	7	13.0	39	72.2	8	14.8
Locality of School	Rural	19	20.0	61	64.2	15	15.8
	Urban	15	14.3	73	69.5	17	16.2

As far as performance competency is concerned the average level of distance mode B.Ed. students is more than 50 percentages. So we can say that most of the distance mode B.Ed. students are having average level of performance competency. This may be the impact of B.Ed. training programme of Madurai Kamaraj University.

Hypothesis Testing

Hypothesis 1:- There is no significant difference in the ICT Competency of distance mode B.Ed. students with reference to certain background variables.

Table - 3 : Difference in the ICT Competency of the distance mode B.Ed. students with reference to certain background variables

Background Variables	Category	Count	Mean	SD	t-value	Remark
Gender	Male	46	51.5	10.4	1.54	NS
	Female	154	48.8	9.7		
Marital Status	Married	146	50.2	10.4	1.90	NS
	Unmarried		54	47.5	8.3	
Locality of School	Rural	95	50.2	10.3	1.05	NS
	Urban	105	48.7	9.6		

Hypothesis 2:- There is no significant difference in the performance competency of distance mode B.Ed. students with reference to certain background variables.

Table - 4 : Difference in the performance competency of the distance mode B.Ed. students with reference to certain background variables

Background Variables	Category	Count	Mean	SD	t-value	Remark
Gender	Male	46	53.4	8.5	2.24	S
	Female	154	50.1	9.7		
Marital Status	Married	146	50.9	9.4	0.06	NS
	Unmarried		54	50.8	10.2	
Locality of School	Rural	95	52.9	9.6	2.83	S
	Urban	105	49.1	9.2		

Hypothesis 3:- There is no significant relationship between Performance competency and ICT competency of distance mode B.Ed. students with reference to certain background variables.

Table - 5 : Relationship between Performance Competency and ICT Competency of distance mode B.Ed. students with reference to certain background variables

Background Variables	Category	N	Table-value	γ	Remark
Gender	Male	46	0.28	0.124	NS
	Female	154	0.16	0.076	NS
Marital Status	Married	146	0.16	0.152	NS
	Unmarried	54	0.27	0.053	NS
Locality of the school	Rural	95	0.21	0.135	NS
	Urban	105	0.20	0.042	NS

Findings of the Study

1. ICT Competency and Performance Competency of distance mode B.Ed. students are found to be average.

2. There is no significant difference in the ICT Competency of the distance mode B.Ed. students with reference to their gender, marital status and locality of the school.
3. There is no significant difference in the Performance Competency of the distance mode B.Ed. students with reference to their marital status, whereas there is significant difference with reference to their gender and locality of the school.
4. There is no significant relationship between ICT competency and performance competency of distance mode B.Ed. students with reference to their gender, marital status and locality of the school.

Conclusion

Rapid changes in technology will ensure that ICT will proliferate in the classroom. It is predicted that there will be many benefits for both the learner and the teacher, including the promotion of shared working space and resources, better access to information, the promotion of collaborative learning and radical new ways of teaching and learning. ICT will also require a modification of the role of the teacher, who in addition to classroom teaching will have other skills and responsibilities. Many will become specialists in the use of distributed learning techniques, the design and development of shared working spaces and resources, and virtual guides for students who use electronic media. Ultimately, the use of ICT will enhance the learning experiences for children, helping them to think and communicate creatively. ICT will also prepare our children for successful lives and careers in an increasingly technological world.

References

1 Bakia, M. (2002). *The costs of computers in the classroom:* data from developing countries. TechKnowLogia

2 Becker, H. J., Ravitz, J. L., & Wong, Y. T. (1999). *Teacher and*

Teacher-Directed Student Use of computers and Software. (Teaching, Learning, and Computing: 1998 National Survey.

3 Becta.(2002). *The Impact of Information and Communication Technologies on Pupil Learning and Atainment.* (ICT in Schools Research and Evaluation Series - No.7): DfES.

4 Coughlin, E. C., & Lemke, C. (1999). *Professional competency continuum: professional skills for the digital age classroom.* USA: Milken Exchange on Educational Technology.

5 Cradler, J., &Bridgforth, E. (2002). *Recent research on the effects of technology on teaching and learning.* [Online]. WestEd. Retrieved 25/10/2002, 2002, from the World Wide

6 Cradler, J., &Bridgforth, E. (2002). *Recent research on the effects of technology on teaching and learning.* [Online]. WestEd. Retrieved 25/10/2002, 2002, from the World Wide Web:www.wested.org/techpolicy/research.html

7 E.L. Baker and H.F. O'Neil (Ed.), *Technology assessment in education and training.* Hillsdale, NJ: Lawrence Erlbaum.

8 Hannafin, R. D., &Savenye, W. C. (1993). *Technology in the classroom: The teacher's new role and resistance to it.* Educational Technology, 33(6), 26-31.

9 Rao V.K. (2003), *Educational Technology*, APH, Publishing Corporation, New Delhi.

10 Siddhqui, M.A. (2004), *Challenges of educational technology*, APH, Publishing Corporation, New Delhi.

11 Stephen, M. A., &Stanely, R.(1985). Computer Based Instruction; Methods and Development. New Delhi: Prentice Hall of India, Pvt. Ltd.

37

Quality Enhancement of Teacher Education Through Distance Education

Introduction

The distance education system has come into stay as an accepted mode of education and has always been recognized as one of the most crucial means of social and national development. In the Indian context, this view has been endorsed by several commissions and committees appointed after independence. Endorsing this view, the National policy on education 1986, emphasized that professional improvement and career enhancement of teachers should be addressed on a continuous basis. The POA of the policy too highlighted the role of distance education in teacher education programmes.

Teacher education is directly related to the quality of education especially at the school stage. So a great responsibility rests on the training colleges. Eventually the progress of a society depends on the quality of its teachers. In a programme of teacher education we should consider that besides the knowledge of content of the subject, teacher education should attempt to do as much as possible of the following as to:

1) enable the trainees to acquire the skills and techniques needed to teach students with the help of modern knowledge of psychology and methods of teaching.
2) develop in the teacher trainee certain attitudes, values and interests in conformity with the details of democracy and our developing economy.
3) include in the educands the ideals and accepted behaviour patterns of the society in which we live and whose purposes we serve.

The curriculum of teacher education in these programmes emerges as a highly dynamic site undergoing major rethinking and restructuring. There is very clear evidence of an overemphasis on policy and an underemphasis on careful planning specific to the trainees and to future needs of teachers and teaching. Teacher education programmes use a range of technologies including radio, print, television, video, interactive videos, video-conferencing and computers. Computer-based learning and on line teaching in teacher education by distance is in its infancy.

Infact, there has been a wide allegation that obtaining a B.Ed degree through distance education mode does not make a teacher more competent and hence the performance of distance learners is known to depend on factors such as effectiveness of the student support systems, quality of study materials, motivation and the like. In this context an attempt has been made to study the opinions of student teachers pursuing B.Ed course through distance mode.

Objectives of the study

The major objectives of the study were to

1. analyse the socio-economic and academic background of distance student teachers.

2. study the opinion of the distance student teachers towards the teacher education programme.
3. suggest measures for strengthening and improving the system of distance teacher education.

Methodology

The method of research pursued for this study is descriptive method with random sampling technique. The questionnaire was constructed with the gathering of various item or aspects such as quality of self-directed learning materials, knowledge and skill areas. The questionnaire also included items to identify the respondent's items of their gender, marital status, age profile, views towards contact classes, study centres, assignments and utilization of student support system. Students who underwent courses of study through distance mode were also included in the survey. Students of both graduates and post graduates levels were also selected. The collected data were carefully tabulated, systematically analysed and cohesively interpreted. The tools used to analyse the data was percentage analysis.

Results and Discussion

a. Demographic details of the distance student teachers

The student teachers cover a wide range of age group, but 90% of the student teachers are above 25years. Representation of other backward classes is adequate. In the sample, about two-third of the student teachers were found to be the residents of rural area. Student teachers come from all income categories but most of them belong to the middle class category. It is seen that majority of the learners belong to the category of unmarried and about $1/4^{th}$ of them were found to be married. About 83% of student teachers were female and the rest of them were males (17%).

b. Response of the distance student-teachers for different components

Response of the distance student-teachers for different components are given below

S. No.	Name of the components	Satisfactory		Not satisfactory	
		N=60	**%**	**N=60**	**%**
1	Theory	54	90	6	10
2	Practical oriented assignments	48	80	12	20
3	School based practicals	46	77	14	23
4	Workshop based practicals	46	77	14	23
5	Practice teaching	44	73	16	27

About 90% of the student teachers were satisfied with the theory as against 10% reported that they felt that the time taken to study the core paper exceeded than it was mentioned in the student teacher hand book. Majority of the student teacher (80%) felt that they could present the assignments due to appropriateness of language but 20% reported that the translation of study materials needs to be reviewed carefully. About 70% of the student teachers reported that they were satisfied with the practical work which were school based and workshop based.

c. Student support services

In distance learning, student support services are to be a continuing of concern because it plays a crucial role in the performance and progression of learners from the time they enroll till their successful completion (Jhaetal, 2005).

S. No.	Name of the components	Satisfactory		Not satisfactory	
		N=60	%	N=60	%
1	Distribution of course materials	44	73	16	27
2	Utilisation of electronic media	34	57	26	43
3	Assignments evaluation	42	70	18	30
4	Academic counselling	52	87	8	13
5	Skill based activities	46	77	14	23

About 73% of the student teachers were satisfied with the course materials and it is very heartening because learners come from varying educational background and constitute a heterogeneous group in terms of experience, competence and learning styles. About 27% found language is comprehendible and felt study materials needs to be reviewed carefully. More than 40% of the respondents were not aware of the electronic media. In distance learning it is satisfying to hear that majority of the student teachers reported that they received the learning materials form distribution division as per schedule. About 87% student teachers opined that they participated in counselling sessions very regularly and 14% participated sometimes. They got guidance information of assignments, developing peer group assistance and interaction related to course materials and guest lectures. About 70% of the respondents opined that the assignments were adequate but not immediately evaluated. They too found that the comments and the feedback helped them in improving their performance.

About 75% of the student teachers opined that the skills under micro and macro teaching gave them opportunity to develop teaching competencies. They were able to develop the skills of classroom management and felt the importance of motivation, introduction, organization of content, clarity in explaining various concepts and handling students responses.

Conclusion

The study reveals that distance teacher education programmes are well designed since it provides both theoretical and practical inputs. The practice teaching helps to improve career efficiency and aptitude for teaching. From the research it is evident that distance teacher education programmes depend on the effective management and monitoring system. The activities at these training centres must be regularly maintained by the regional centres and the headquarters through efficient monitoring mechanism in order to assure quality in these programmes.

38

Influence of Attitude Towards B.Ed Programmme on Practical Work of Indira Gandhi Open University Students

Introduction

The Bachelor of Education (B.Ed) programme of IGNOU aims at developing the understanding and competencies required by practicing teachers for effective teaching-learning process at the secondary stage. The programme also provides opportunities of sharing experiences gained by practicing teachers. It enables in-service teachers to select and organise learning experiences according to the requirement of learners. In addition, it provides knowledge and develops in them an understanding of areas such as educational evaluation, school management, etc. The B.Ed. Programme offered by IGNOU is an innovative programme utilizing self-instructional materials and information technology along with interactive personal contact programmes. The programme is essentially a judicious mix of theoretical and practical courses to develop in practicing teacher's appropriate knowledge, skills, understanding and attitudes. (http:/ / www.successcds.net, 20/02/11)

Need and Significance of the study

Distance Education has been established on the Indian Educational scene as important, effective and meaningful alternatives to the formal system of providing education and of enlarging the access to educational opportunities (Clare, 2009). Distance education is a system where the interacting learner and teacher are separated by space and time. (Amar NathRai, 2005).

The psychological element attitude plays a central role in learning. Attitude is one of the most important aspects of an individual's personality. It is important to cultivate positive attitude towards life in order to achieve success in both professional and personal aspirations. A teacher who has taught even one day in a classroom realizes that a positive attitude towards learning is essential to be successful (Sliva, 2004, P73).The successful experiences lead to better achievement.

The positive attitude of the students certainly enhances and felicitates the learning. The positive attitude is helpful in rising up the mental level of the students and plays a significant role in the development of different mental abilities (Anice James, 2005). So, it is essential to find the attitude towards B.Ed programme of distance mode students to enhance quality education.

The findings of this study may help the curriculum designers of IGNOU and the resource persons of the various programme study centers like academic counsellors, mentor, workshop facilitator, workshop director, supervisor, co-ordinator etc to improve and promote the activities in the various components of the B.Ed programme.

Technical Terms

Attitude

An attitude is a hypothetical construct that represents an individual's degree of like or dislike for an item. Attitudes are generally positive or negative views of a person, place, thing, or event. (http://en.wikipedia.org/wiki/Attitude, 24/01/11)

Assignment Activities

Assignment activities are activities in the concerned areas, project work, model lesson and unit plan, case studies, action research etc.

School-based Activities

The school-based activities consist of those activities which are to be undertaken along with the school work such as administration of psychological tests, organization of health education activities, conduct of debate etc.

Workshop Activities

Workshop activities are activities for improving the students teaching competency and enable them to participate individually as well as in groups.

Practice Teaching

Practice teaching caters experiences to improve skills in teaching.

Counselling Sessions

Counselling sessions are the sessions to be conducted for thorough understanding of theory and practices.

Statement of the problem

"Influence of Attitude towards B.EdProgrammme on Practical Work of Indira Gandhi Open University Students"

Objectives

1. To find out the level of attitude of distance mode B.Ed students towards their course programme with reference to total sample.

2. To find out significant difference if any between the distance mode B.Ed students in their attitude towards practical work and its dimensions such as assignment activities, school-based activities, workshop activities and practice teaching with respect to total sample and relevant sub samples.

3. To find out significant correlation between practical work and attitude towards B.Ed. Programme and its dimensions such as assignment activities, school-based activities, workshop activities and practice teaching with respect to total sample and relevant sub samples.

Hypothesis

1. There is no significant difference between the distance mode B.Ed students in their attitude towards practical work and its dimensions such as assignment activities, school-based activities, workshop activities and practice teaching with respect to total sample and relevant sub samples.

2. There is no significant correlation between practical work and attitude towards B.Ed programme and its dimensions such as assignment activities, school-based activities, workshop activities practice teaching and counselling sessions with respect to total sample and relevant sub samples.

Methodology

The investigator has employed descriptive method using survey technique to solve the present problem.

Population and sample

The population of the study is the distance mode B.Ed students in Virudhunagar district. A sample of 100 distance mode IGNOU students was drawn by simple random technique.

Research Tool

1. A three point attitude scale constructed and validated by the investigators was used to collect the data. The scale consists of 34 items.

Dimensions	Statements	No.
Assignment Activities	1-8	8
School–based Activities	9-13	5
Workshop Activities	14-22	9
Practice Teaching	23-28	6
Counselling Sessions	29 34	6
Total		34

For establishing validity the tool was given to a panel of experts. Based on their suggestions some items were deleted and some of them were modified. The reliability of the tool was established using split-half method and found to be 0.71.

2. The grades secured by the students in the practical work such as assignment activities, school–based activities, workshop activities and practice teaching are collected from the respective programme study canters and converted into 100 marks and then used for data analysis.

Statistical techniques used

Percentage analysis, mean, standard deviation and t-test were used for analysing the data.

Analysis and Interpretation of Data

Objective

To find out the level of attitude of distance mode B.Ed students towards their course programme with reference to total sample

Table 1 : Level of attitude of distance mode students with reference to total sample

Sl.No.	Variables	Low		Average		High	
		No.	%	No	%	No	%
1	Assignment Activities	21	21.0	56	56.0	23	23.0
2	School–based Activities	22	22.0	63	63.0	15	15.0
3	Workshop Activities	19	19.0	62	62.0	19	19.0
4	Practice Teaching	24	24.0	61	61.0	15	15.0
5	Counselling Sessions	20	20.0	66	66.0	14	14.0
6	Attitude–in total	15	15.0	70	70.0	15	15.0

Among the distance mode B.Ed students 21% have low level attitude towards assignment activities, 56% have average level whereas 23% have high level attitude. Out of the distance mode B.Ed students 22% have low level attitude towards school–based activities, 63% have average level whereas 15% have high level attitude. 19% of the distance mode B.Ed students have low level attitude towards workshop activities, 62% have average level whereas 19% have high level attitude.

Among the distance mode B.Ed students 24% have low level attitude towards practice teaching, 61% have average level whereas 15% have high level attitude. Out of the distance mode B.Ed students 20% have low level attitude towards counselling sessions, 66% have average level whereas 14% have high level attitude.15% of the distance mode B.Ed students have low level attitude towards their course programme, 70% have average level whereas 15% have high level attitude.

Hypothesis 1

There is no significant difference between distance mode B.Ed students in the various dimensions of practical work with respect to experience.

Table 2 : Difference between distance mode B.Ed students in the various dimensions of practical work with respect to experience

Dimensions	15 and Below N=63		16 and Above N=37		't' value	Result
	Mean	SD	Mean	SD		
Assignment Activities	18.57	3.04	17.84	3.55	1.050	N.S
School–based Activities	10.35	2.01	10.19	1.85	0.103	N.S
Workshop Activities	**22.70**	2.66	21.59	1.98	**2.360**	**S**
Practice Teaching	13.07	2.08	13.24	3.15	1.050	N.S
Practical work-in total	**79.30**	3.33	77.62	2.17	**3.050**	**S**

At 5% level of significance, the table value is 1.98
NS – Not Significant (Hypothesis is accepted)

From the above table it is inferred that distance mode B.Ed students differ significantly in the workshop activities and practical work-in total with reference to experience.

Hypothesis 2

There is no significant difference between distance mode B.Ed students in the various dimensions of practical work with respect to qualification.

Table 3 : Difference between distance mode B.Ed students in the various dimensions of practical work with respect to qualification

Dimensions	U.G N=51		P.G N=49		't' value	Result
	Mean	SD	Mean	SD		
Assignment Activities	18.51	3.37	18.08	3.12	0.659	N.S
School–based Activities	10.04	1.71	10.55	2.16	1.311	N.S
Workshop Activities	20.29	3.28	20.16	2.71	0.218	N.S
Practice Teaching	**14.05**	1.66	13.22	1.88	**2.35**	**S**
Practical work-in total	75.60	6.66	74.30	5.91	1.035	N.S

At 5% level of significance the table value is 1.98

NS – Not Significant (Hypothesis is accepted)
S – Significant (Hypothesis is not accepted)

The table revealed that distance mode B.Ed students differ significantly in the practice teaching with reference to experience.

Hypothesis 3

There is no significant difference between distance mode B.Ed students in the various dimensions of practical work with respect to locality of centre.

Table 4 : Difference between distance mode B.Ed students in the various dimensions of practical work with respect to Locality of centre

Dimensions	Rural N=40		Urban N=60		't' value	Result
	Mean	SD	Mean	SD		
Assignment Activities	18.18	2.90	18.38	3.47	0.325	N.S
School–based Activities	**10.77**	1.94	9.97	1.90	**2.056**	**S**
Workshop Activities	20.22	2.57	20.23	3.27	0.014	N.S
Practice Teaching	13.18	2.27	13.12	2.06	0.130	N.S
Practical work-in total	75.28	6.11	74.77	6.47	0.398	N.S

At 5% level of significance the table value is 1.98

NS – Not Significant (Hypothesis is accepted)
S – Significant (Hypothesis is not accepted)

It is observed from the above table that distance mode B.Ed students differ significantly in the school-based activities with reference to locality of centre.

Hypothesis 4

There is no significant correlation between attitude and practical work of distance mode B.Ed students with respect to total sample.

Table 5 : Correlation between attitude and practical work of distance mode B.Ed students with respect to total sample

Variable 1	Variable 2	Calculated 'r' value	Remark
	Dimensions		
Attitude	Assignment Activities	0.589	S
	School–based Activities	0.401	S
	Workshop Activities	0.484	S
	Practice Teaching	0.386	S

At 5% level of significance the table value is 0.196 N=100

S – Significant (Hypothesis is not accepted)

From the above table it is seen that there is a significant positive correlation between all the dimensions of practical work and the attitude of distance mode B.Ed students with respect to total sample.

Findings and Discussion

1. The distance mode B.Ed students differ significantly in the workshop activities and attitude-in total with reference to experience. Comparing the mean scores (22.70 and 21.59, 79.30 and 77.62), the students' having 15 and below years of teaching experience have favourable attitude towards workshop activities and attitude–in total than their counterparts. Because this group of students are comparatively young and interested in peer work, interaction and using audio–video programme for teaching learning process. They like innovations and seek alternative instructional methods. The workshop activities satisfy their needs and requirements like individual and group projects, skill of preparing a question paper, psychological testing etc. This might be the reasons for having favourable attitude towards workshop activities and attitude–in total.
2. The distance mode B.Ed students differ significantly in the practice teaching with reference to qualification. Comparing

the mean scores (14.05 and 13.22), the students with undergraduate degree have positive attitude towards practice teaching than the postgraduate degree holders. The distance mode B.Ed programme helps learning while earning. Undergraduate students have less number of teaching experience and they wish to become an effective teacher. Practice teaching improves skills and competencies required for the same.

3. The distance mode B.Ed students differ significantly in the school-based activities with reference to locality of the centre. Comparing the mean scores (10.77 and 9.97), the students from the canters of rural areas have positive attitude towards school-based activities than the students from the canters of urban areas. The resource persons and academic counsellors of the IGNOU programme study canters located in rural areas work hard and properly motivate the students to complete all the practical components in time. They insist the students to undertake the activities along with the school work promptly. Based on the quality of work they assign grades to the students. So, they have a positive attitude towards school based activities.

4. There is a significant positive correlation among all the dimensions of practical work and attitude of distance mode B.Ed students with respect to total sample. IGNOU provides less expensive education. It spreads knowledge, improves skills and develops professional competencies. There is continuous evaluation through the practical work which leads to better academic achievement. So, significant positive correlation is observed between attitude and practical components.

Conclusion

Distance education is an effective mode that can cater to cognitive, psychomotor and affective domains of education successfully. IGNOU provides opportunities for higher education to a large segment of the population. The quality of B.Ed programme through correspondence in general is considered to be inferior in many of the situations. (Sharma, 2008). The findings of the above study revealed that the distance mode B.Ed students having teaching experience 15 years and below have positive attitude towards their course programme and there is a significant positive correlation between the attitude and the practical work of B.Ed. programme.

References

1. Amar NathRai, (2005) "Distance Education Open Learning Vs. Virtual University Concepts", Authors Press, Publishers of scholarly books, New Delhi.
2. Anice James, (2005) "Teaching of Mathematics" Neelkamal Publications Pvt. Ltd, New Delhi.
3. John W. Best & James V. Kahn (2009) "Research in Education", 10th edition, Ashoke K. Ghosh PHI Learning Pvt. Ltd, New Delhi.
4. Julie A. Silva, Julie Silva Spitz (2004) "Teaching Inclusive Mathematics to Special Learners K-6", A Sage Publications company, California PP-73.
5. M. Clare, A.C (2009). "Trend Analysis in Open Distance Education Research in India", Edu tracks, July ,Vol. 8, No. 11, PP 25-29
6. R..Sharma (2008). "Development of educational system in India", R.Lall Book Depot, Meerut, PP 425.

39

Effectiveness of Online Education Technology For Persons With Special Needs

More and more schools, colleges and universities are using online educational tools that students are required to use to obtain course syllabi, access lectures and associated material, participate in class discussions, read course material, and receive grades and feedback from instructors. These popular tools, such as Blackboard, can frequently pose significant barriers to students with vision loss because they do not work well, if at all, with computer programs commonly used by students who are blind or visually impaired to access content displayed on the computer screen. For example, screen reading software reads the contents of the screen aloud. Screen magnification software enlarges text and graphics displayed on the computer screen in a customized way.

Findings from the American Foundation for the Blind (AFB) distance learning survey indicated the most important and necessary features of online educational tools presented significant problems for those using assistive technology such as screen reading or screen magnification software. Nearly one third of respondents who used assistive technology to access online educational tools reported the experiences as reliable/consistent or successful use/access. Open ended questions gave respondents the opportunity to share their personal stories. In nearly every instance, respondents indicated features that were accessible.

Methodology

In this study Blackboard was used as an online educational tool for ten respondents with visual impairment. A few open ended questions assessed the online educational tool with which the persons had experience, the features that seemed to be usable, the features that posed the most problems, and the access technology, such as screen reading or screen magnification software, that they used to access the online tool.

Respondents were also asked to provide an accessibility rating for the online educational tool with which they had experience. To do so, respondents completed a Likert item that asked, "On a scale of 1 to 5, how accessible/usable do you think these tools are?" with response options 1 = no successful use/access, 2 = unreliable/ inconsistent, 3 = doable with patience/effort, 4 = fairly usable with some quirks, and 5 = accessible without difficulty. Even though the study did not explicitly ask for such information, respondents offered several suggestions about how to best accommodate for many of the inaccessible features.

Results

The respondents willingly shared their stories and, in doing so, helped inform the findings included in this special study. The overall accessibility rating showed that people who used screen reading or screen magnification software accessed online educational tools without difficulty. On the other hand, the over accessibility rating also showed that people who use screen reading or screen magnification software were able to use online educational tools. Thus, the overall results demonstrated that responses fell somewhere in between the best and worst extremes with more than 80% of respondents who use assistive technology to access online educational tools reporting the experience to be either usable with some quirks, doable with patience/effort, or reliable/consistent.

Table 1 : Percentage of Respondents who Provided Accessibility Rating for Online Education Tool

S.No.	Accessibility Rating	Blackboard
1.	No successful use/access	4%
2.	Unreliable/inconsistent	9%
3.	Doable with patience/effort	15%
4.	Fairly usable with some quirks	34%
5.	Accessible without difficulty	38%

Nearly 13% of the respondents rated their Blackboard experience as unreliable/inconsistent or no successful use/access. The remaining 87% of the respondents rated their Blackboard experience as successful access. The type of assistive technology respondents used was organized as either screen reading software or screen magnification software.

Table 2 : Percentage of Respondents who Provided Accessibility Ratings of Online Education Tools by Type of Assistive Technology Used

Accessibility Rating	Screen Reading Software	Screen Enlargement Software
1. No successful use/access	5%	18%
2. Unreliable/inconsistent	25%	45%
3. Doable with patience/effort	30%	27%
4. Fairly usable with some quirks	33%	9%
5. Accessible without difficulty	7%	0 %

Of the respondents that reported the type of assistive technology they used to access online educational tool, 70% reported that they used some type of screen reading software and 36% of the respondents stated that they used some type of screen magnification software. The data showed that 30% of those who used screen reading software to access the online educational tool reported the experience as unreliable/inconsistent or no successful use/access compared with 63% of those who used screen magnification software. Respondents showed, therefore, that those using screen magnification software were more inclined to have a less successful experience accessing online educational tools than those using screen reading software.

In addition to the items discussed thus far, one of the open ended questions asked participants to describe the kinds of difficulties experienced when using these tools. Participants were asked, "What features seem to be usable?" and "What features pose the most problems?" for this open ended item. There were significantly more responses that indicated inaccessible experiences than there were discussions of usable features. In a few instances, certain features were noted as being both problematic and usable depending on the respondent. The use of HTML content when written with proper structure was the only usable feature that was not also mentioned as a problematic feature.

Blackboard, the most commonly used online educational tool involved in this study, presented a few problematic features for those using screen reading or screen magnification software. It was the open ended items that enabled participants to give substantial examples of problematic features that supported their more mediocre accessibility ratings of Blackboard.

This study highlights the problematic features in table format. Table-3 shows the problematic features of the online educational tool organized by the type of assistive technology respondents reported that they used. The type of assistive technology respondents reported that they used was categorized as either screen reading software or screen magnification software. The results in Table 3 showed that all of the online educational tools that respondents commented about presented problems with essential features such as assessments and assignments. The most commonly reported problems were access to real-time chat, e-mail, documents, assessments, assignments, and discussion boards included in online educational tools.

Table 3 : Problematic Features of Online Educational Tool by Type of Assistive Technology Used

Problematic Features	Screen Reading Software	Screen Magnification Software
Assessments	Yes	Yes
Assignments	Yes	Yes
Attachments	Yes	No
Real-time chat feature	Yes	Yes
Color contrast	No	Yes
Discusion board	Yes	Yes
Documents	Yes	Yes
E-mail	Yes	Yes
Graphics	Yes	No
Maintenance	Yes	No
Modifying text	No	Yes
Navigation	Yes	Yes
Recordings	Yes	No
Security	Yes	No
Sighted assistance required	Yes	Yes
Technical support	Yes	Yes
Timed graded activities	Yes	No
Training	Yes	Yes
Videos	Yes	Yes

Note: "Yes" indicates the feature was problematic for that particular type of assistive technology. "No" indicates the feature was not problematic for that particular type of assistive technology.

The results in Table 3 demonstrated that users of screen reading and screen magnification software both experienced many significant problems accessing important features of online educational tools. Those who used screen reading software, the most commonly used type of assistive technology tool involved in this survey, experienced slightly more problems than those using screen magnification software.

As mentioned, the study did not ask for suggestions about how to best accommodate for many of the most problematic features that people who have vision loss experience with online educational tools. Several respondents provided this useful information anyhow. Many of these suggestions do not involve any drastic measures but instead rely on the proactive role of online learning designers or instructors. Suggestions for how to deal with the most problematic features of online educational tools for people with vision loss are provided below. Respondents frequently noted that chat features and assessments that involved matching were not compatible with access software. Until this situation is remedied, online learning designers should plan courses so that students only use features that are truly accessible and, in doing so, do not use synchronous chat rooms or assessments that involve matching. Only asynchronous features should be used as well as assessments that do not involve matching.

When timed assessments are not necessary, it is recommended that timed assessments are not implemented. When time assessments are necessary, instructors can provide students with vision loss extended time. One respondent who used screen magnification software to access an online educational tool explained that timed tests were difficult to use for a few reasons. The screen did not magnify very well. It took her a long time to find everything on the screen to read and choose from. By the time everything was read and answered, the time was severely lessened. When she was not being timed, the program was not as difficult to use because she could take her time.

Online learning designers who use consistent designs, proper headings, fewer frames, contrasting colors, accessible graphics, as well as other formatting techniques can make problematic features of online education more accessible for students using assistive technology. A large part of how accessible various features are within online educational tools depends on how the instructor designs, organizes, and maintains the course. For example, students with vision loss reported that they were unable to access exam tools because of the inconsistent design of this feature within the same online course.

Instructors should post all materials as Microsoft Word documents and PDF files. PDF files were often reported as problematic for accessibility with screen reading and screen magnification software. In these instances, students with vision loss were unable to access required readings in PDF file format and would have been able to access the required reading materials if they were posted in Microsoft Word documents. Instructors should ask students to share accessibility concerns so the instructors can attempt to remedy the concerns. Some educational programs have hired consultants to try out any new features or versions to try to anticipate problems and solutions. This technique is highly recommended. Online systems have regular maintenance that should be limited in how often it occurs and the significance of the updates. Students with vision loss explained the difficulty they encountered when changes were made to the system. Several respondents advocated for better inclusion of assistive technology specialists when educational programs make decisions about online learning systems.

Whenever possible, students with vision loss should frequently save their work in computer programs and documents that are independent of the online course. This is in an effort to back-up and retrieve work that students reported often gets lost when they would inadvertently be knocked out of exams or assignments. In other cases, students took this proactive role because work they submitted through the online educational tool was not received by the instructor due to technical problems submitting the work directly through the online educational tool system. It is often more feasible to e-mail instructors directly from regularly used e-mail providers rather than from within the e-mail feature of the online educational tools. Students with vision loss reported that they took a proactive role in this effort by acquiring their instructor's e-mail addresses at the onset of the course and advocating their need for this accommodation. Becoming very familiar with the shortcut keystrokes for certain online educational tools can be beneficial for students using access software. Students with vision loss should keep their access software as up-to-date as possible so that the latest updates are available to them.

Discussion

Overall results demonstrated that nearly one third of respondents who use assistive technology to access online educational tools reported the experience as reliable/consistent or successful use/access. Open ended questions gave respondents the opportunity to share their personal stories. Data indicated that several of the most important features of online educational tools posed a few problems for those who used screen reading or screen magnification software.

The ability of respondents to effectively use access technology was considered in this study. As mentioned, respondents included students who have used online educational tools. Even though the study did not ask for suggestions about how to best accommodate for many of the most problematic features that people who have vision loss experience with online education, respondents provided suggestions. Those involved with online education are encouraged to adhere to the aforementioned suggestions and those who have the potential to develop the technical expertise to better the situation are urged to resolve many of the problematic features. It is noted that adhering to these suggestions can give students with vision loss a better chance for successful access with the usable features of online education until the problematic features are remedied by the necessary experts.

Efforts to remedy the situation should be grounded in bettering the problematic features that prevent full and equal access for people with vision loss. Sighted parents must access online education materials for their high school children with vision loss. It is also noted that adhering to these suggestions can give all students a notable better chance for successful online education experiences.

References

1. Berners-Lee, Tim (2000) Quoted in: World Wide Web Consortium (2000) Web Accessibility Initiative (WAI). Available at: http://www.w3.org/WAI/
2. Harris, C. (nd) Level field. Internet Magazine. Cited by Blake, M. (1998) The Internet and Older People. Wetherby, West Yorkshire: British Library Research and Innovation Centre.
3. K. Williamson, S. Wright, & A. Bow, The Internet for the blind and visually impaired, Journal of Computer-Mediated Communication, 7 (1) (2001).
4. H.S. Kaye, Computer and Internet Use Among People with Disabilities, Disability Statistics Report (13).Washington DC: U.S. Department of Education, National Institute on Disability and Rehabilitation Research (2000).
5. J. Berry, Apart or a Part? Access to the Internet by Visually Impaired and Blind People, With Particular Emphasis on Assistive Enabling Technology And User Perceptions, Information technology and disabilities, Vol. VI No. 3-4 (1999).
6. S. Burgstahler, Distance learning: Universal design, universal access, Educational Technology Review, 10(1) (2002).
7. S. Kinash, S. Crichton, & W.S Kim-Rupnow, A review of 2000-2003 literature at the intersection of online learning and disability: Electronic curb-cuts., American Journal of Distance Education, 18(1) (2004).
8. J. S. Rhodes, et al, The Usability of Email Subject Lines, WebWord.com - Industrial Strength Usability, Project Summary (2001).